Leadership and Strategic Management in Education

This book, *Leadership and Strategic Management in Education*, is the reader for one of the core modules of the MBA in Educational Management offered by the EDMU, University of Leicester.

The other modules in this course are:

Managing Finance and External Relations
Human Resource Management in Schools and Colleges
Managing the Curriculum
Research Methods in Educational Management

For further information about the MBA in Educational Management, please contact the EMDU at emdu@le.ac.uk. For further information about the books associated with the course, contact Paul Chapman Publishing at http://www.sagepub.co.uk.

EDUCATIONAL
MANAGEMENT
DEVELOPMENT
UNIT

Leadership and Strategic Management in Education

Tony Bush and Marianne Coleman
EMDU, University of Leicester

P·CP

Paul Chapman
Publishing Ltd

Paul Chapman Publishing Ltd
A SAGE Publications Company
6 Bonhill Street
London EC2A 4PU

SAGE Publications Inc
2455 Teller Road
Thousand Oaks, California 91320

SAGE Publications India Pvt Ltd
32, M-Block Market
Greater Kailash – I
New Delhi 110 048

British Cataloguing in Publication data

A catalogue record for this book is available from the British Library

ISBN 0 7619 6872 5
ISBN 0 7619 6873 3 (pbk)

Library of Congress catalog card number available

601326

Typeset by PDQ Typesetting, Newcastle-under-Lyme, Staffordshire
Printed and bound in Great Britain by the Cromwell Press, Wiltshire
A B C D E F 3 2 1 0 9 8

Contents

The authors

Tony Bush and **Marianne Coleman** both work in the Educational Management Development Unit of Leicester University, based in Northampton.

Professor Tony Bush is Director of the EMDU. His major publications include: *Theories of Educational Management* (second edition) (1995), Paul Chapman Publishing; *The Principles of Educational Management* (1994), with J. West-Burnham, Longman; *Managing People in Education* (1997), with D. Middlewood, Paul Chapman Publishing; *Educational Management: Redefining Theory, Policy and Practice* (1999), with L. Bell, R. Bolam, R. Glatter and P. Ribbins, Paul Chapman Publishing.

Dr Marianne Coleman is a senior lecturer and Director of Distance Learning in the EMDU. Her major publications include: *Managing Autonomous Schools: The Grant-Maintained Experience* (1993), with T. Bush and D. Glover, Paul Chapman Publishing; *Practitioner Research in Education: Making a Difference* (1999), with D. Middlewood and J. Lumby, Paul Chapman Publishing; 'The management style of female headteachers' (1996), *Educational Management and Administration*, Vol. 24, no. 2; 'Barriers to career progress for women in education: the perception of female headteachers' (1996), *Educational Research*, Vol. 38, no. 3. 'The female secondary headteacher in England and Wales: leadership and management styles (2000) *Educational Research* Vol. 42, no. 1.

Acknowledgements

The authors' thanks go to the support staff of the EMDU for all their help and assistance in the completion of the manuscript.

1. Introduction

This book is intended primarily for students taking advanced courses in educational management, such as Leicester University's Educational Management Development Unit's MBA in Educational Management. It is therefore written as a teaching text. However, it also offers much to the general reader, especially those working in education, in terms of an opportunity to increase their understanding and knowledge of, and develop their skills in aspects of, educational management.

The specific aims of this book are to:

- equip readers with a body of knowledge that will improve their understanding of leadership and strategic management;
- enable readers to reflect on concepts, theories and models of management in education;
- provide a range of analytical frameworks that can be applied by readers to their own working environments;
- provide opportunities for the improvement of their skills in leadership and strategic management through site-based research; and
- enable readers to contribute to school or college improvement.

By the end of this book, readers should be able to:

- appreciate the relationship between theory and practice in education;
- understand the concepts of strategy, vision and mission;
- distinguish between effectiveness, improvement and quality;
- understand theories of leadership; and
- apply concepts of leadership and strategic management to their own management practice.

❏ Activities
Throughout the book you will find activities which ask you to:

- analyse and reflect on what you have read;
- examine and criticise practice constructively; and
- develop explanations to test the relationship between theory and practice.

These activities help you to reflect upon what you have read and relate it to your own management practice, now and in the future. They may also assist you when you are considering a specific topic to investigate for a written assignment.

❏ Linked reading
This text is free-standing and contains ample material for the reader to be able to improve his or her management practice or produce a course assignment or project. However, additional reading is clearly helpful, and for students essential. There are two key books to draw to your attention:

1. Middlewood, D. and Lumby, J. (eds.) (1998) *Strategic Management in Schools and Colleges*, London, Paul Chapman Publishing. All the chapters from this volume are relevant to your study and you will be asked to read certain chapters at specific points in the text.

2. Bush, T. and West-Burnham, J. (eds.) (1994) *The Principles of Educational Management*, Harlow, Longman. The following chapters are particularly relevant to this book and you may wish to read them through quickly before starting: Chapter 1 (John West-Burnham) – 'Management in

educational organizations'; Chapter 2 (Tony Bush) – 'Theory and practice in educational management'; Chapter 3 (Marianne Coleman) – 'Leadership in educational management'; Chapter 4 (John West-Burnham) – 'Strategy, policy and planning'; Chapter 5 (John O'Neill) – 'Organisational structure and culture'.

The following chapters are also relevant: Chapter 9 (Marianne Coleman) – 'Women in educational management'; Chapter 15 (Tony Bush) – 'Accountability in education'.

The references provide an additional source which may be helpful in preparing assignments.

❑ Structure of this book

Chapter 2 provides an introduction to the concepts of leadership and strategic management in education and provides some definitions of key terms. Chapter 3 examines three principles, vision, mission and strategy, which are often used to describe and explain the purposes of educational organisations. In Chapter 4, we explore the concept of leadership and assess its importance in education, consider gender issues in educational management and the concept of leadership roles. In Chapter 5, we explore the relationship between organisational theory and strategic management and demonstrate the links between theory and practice in education.

Chapter 6 examines three central concepts, effectiveness, improvement and quality, which have been increasingly applied to the management of schools and colleges. Chapter 7 discusses strategic and development planning in education and links these processes to improvement and effectiveness. We conclude, in Chapter 8, with a discussion of the need to manage strategic change.

2. Strategic management in education

This chapter considers:

- the nature and purpose of educational management;
- the shift to self-management for schools and colleges; and
- strategy and self-management.

Introduction

The importance of effective management in educational organisations has been increasingly recognised. Schools and colleges are likely to be much more effective in providing a good education for their pupils and students if they are well managed. The research on school effectiveness and school improvement in many countries shows that the quality of leadership and management is one of the most important variables in distinguishing between successful and unsuccessful schools (Sammons *et al.*, 1994). This finding means that management cannot be a 'taken for granted' aspect of educational institutions. Good management makes a difference to the quality of schools and colleges and to the educational outcomes of their students.

The introduction of self-managing schools and colleges in many countries, including Australia, England and Wales, Hong Kong, Israel, New Zealand and the USA, has also increased the importance of effective school and college management. This is because schools have taken responsibility for many functions that were previously undertaken by national, regional or local government. These often include financial management, most aspects of staff management and the management of links with groups external to the school or college. Now that educational organisations have direct responsibility for most aspects of management, it is possible for leaders to adopt a strategic approach, integrating several different aspects of management to set and achieve goals.

Strategic management can be distinguished from operational, or day-to-day, management in two respects.

❏ Scope
Strategy requires an overview of the organisation which encompasses all its activities. Managers seek to integrate tasks so that they are consistent with the values of the school and are mutually compatible. It is a holistic approach and not confined to specific departments or subunits.

❏ Timetable
Strategy requires an extended timescale. It is long-term management not simply a response to current events. Typically it will extend over a period of years and be reflected in development planning.

Management is not confined to the headteacher/principal or chief executive. Management is dispersed amongst those responsible for curriculum development and student pastoral care. However, strategic management is usually exercised by the principal and the senior management team (SMT) working with the governing body.

Leadership and management

The terms 'leadership' and 'management' are sometimes used interchangeably or regarded as synonyms. This is justifiable in so far as these activities are often carried out in schools and colleges by the same people, and often at the same time. In the 1990s, however, a distinction has been drawn between these two concepts. Leadership is sometimes linked to vision and values while management is said to relate to processes and structures. Leadership has been identified by some, for example by the chief executive of the Teacher Training Agency in England and Wales, as the most important aspect for successful schools while management has been relegated to a secondary position: 'The central issue we need to tackle is leadership, in particular how the qualities of leadership can be identified and fostered' (Millett, 1996).

The present authors take a different view, believing that the distinction between leadership and management is often overdrawn and that both are equally important for educational effectiveness:

> Organisations which are over managed but under led eventually lose any sense of spirit or purpose. Poorly managed organisations with strong charismatic leaders may soar temporarily only to crash shortly thereafter. The challenge of modern organisations requires the objective perspective of the manager as well as the brilliant flashes of vision and commitment wise leadership provides (Bolman and Deal, 1991, pp. xiii–xiv).

> Methods…[are] as important as knowledge, understanding and value orientations… Erecting this kind of dichotomy between something pure called 'leadership' and something 'dirty' called 'management', or between values and purposes on the one hand and methods and skills on the other, would be disastrous (Glatter, 1997, p. 189).

Effective leadership **and** management are required to generate school improvement. We turn now to consider the nature of management in education. Leadership is considered in detail in Chapter 4.

What is educational management?

Educational management is a field of study and practice concerned with the operation of educational organisations (Bush, 1995). There is no single generally accepted definition of the subject because of its diverse conceptual origins that will be reflected in the next chapter. The following examples suggest some commonalities but there are clear differences of emphasis:

> Management is a continuous process through which members of an organisation seek to co-ordinate their activities and utilise their resources in order to fulfil the various tasks of the organisation as efficiently as possible (Hoyle, 1981, p. 8).

> [Management] is an activity involving responsibility for getting things done through other people (Cuthbert, 1984, p. 37).

> [Management is concerned with] the internal operation of educational institutions, and also with their relationships with their environment, that is, the communities in which they are set, and with the governing bodies to which they are formally responsible (Glatter, 1979, p. 16).

Everard and Morris (1990, p. 4) identify five stages of management:

a) Setting direction, aims and objectives.
b) Planning how progress will be made or a goal achieved.
c) Organising available resources (people, time, materials) so that the goal can be achieved in the planned way.
d) Controlling the process (i.e. measuring achievement against the plan and taking corrective action where appropriate).

e) Setting and improving organisational standards.

These stages could apply to the work of any teacher but, as Cuthbert's definition implies, management generally relates to working with other staff. Heads and principals, and members of SMTs, would generally be regarded as senior managers while heads of department or subject leaders, together with heads of year, are middle managers. Classroom teachers with no other role would not be thought of as managers of other staff.

Activity

Which teachers should be regarded as managers in primary schools?

❏ Comment

In most British primary schools, only the headteacher has time specifically allocated for management. Deputy heads and subject co-ordinators are usually full-time class teachers. However, they still fulfil the definition of management discussed above. While the lack of time available for management tasks is a problem, their subject responsibilities mean they should still be regarded as managers. In many schools, all staff have subject responsibilities and thus have management duties.

In some other countries, notably China, Hong Kong and Singapore, primary schools are generally larger than in Britain and subject leaders are generally titled 'Head of Department'. These middle managers also have some non-contact time allocated for their management roles.

◎ Reading

Please read pages 11–18 of John West-Burnham's 'Management in educational organizations', Chapter 1 in Bush, T. and West-Burnham, J. (eds.) *Principles of Educational Management.*

West-Burnham considers several aspects of educational management in this chapter. The main issues addressed are:

1. **Educational management is a relatively new subject, dating from about 1970.**
2. **The confused nomenclature of the subject with overlapping terms: policy, management, administration and leadership.**
3. **The origins of theory in educational management and the links between theory and practice.**

The purpose of educational management

The first aspect of management identified by Everard and Morris (above) is 'setting direction, aims and objectives'. A clear goal orientation is central to many of the theoretical approaches to educational management, as we shall see later. Two examples illustrate this point:

> Defining purpose is a central function of administration (Culbertson, 1983, quoted in Bush, 1995, p.1).

> An organisation is developed to achieve certain goals or objectives by group activity (Cyert, 1975, quoted in Bush, 1995, p. 2).

At a general level, defining purpose in education is straightforward; it has to relate to learning. A simple example is given below:

> The purpose of educational management is to facilitate student learning and in doing so to serve as a model for the learning process.

The issues here are of integrity and consistency – the management of schools and colleges should be logically derived from their core purpose and provide a clear exemplar of those principles at work. We can sum this up with the old saying 'Practise what you preach'.

In practice, however, there are real difficulties in moving beyond this uncontentious starting point. Three aspects of goal-setting may be problematic:

- The value *of formal* statements of purpose.
- Whether the objectives are those of the organisation or those of particular individuals.
- *How* the institution's goals are determined.

❏ Formal aims

The formal aims of schools and colleges tend to be rather vague and general. They usually command substantial support but often provide an inadequate basis for managerial action. A typical aim in a primary or secondary school might focus on the acquisition by each pupil of physical, social, intellectual and moral qualities and skills. This is worthy but it has considerable limitations as a guide to decision-making. More specific purposes often fail to reach the same level of agreement. A proposal to seek improved performance in mathematics and science, for example, may be challenged by teachers concerned about the implications for other subjects.

❏ Organisational or individual aims

Some approaches to educational management are concerned predominantly with *organisational* objectives while other models strongly emphasise *individual* aims. There is a range of opinion between these two views. Gray (1979, p. 12) stresses both elements: 'the management process is concerned with helping the members of an organisation to attain individual as well as organisational objectives within the changing environment of the organisation'. A potential problem is that individual and organisational objectives may be incompatible or that organisational aims satisfy some, but not all, individual aspirations. It is reasonable to assume that most teachers want their school or college to pursue policies which are in harmony with their own interests and preferences. Conflict may result if school policies contradict the values and aims of a large group of teachers.

❏ The determination of aims

The process of deciding on the aims of the organisation is at the heart of educational management. In some settings, aims are decided by the headteacher or principal, often working in association with senior colleagues. In many schools and colleges, however, goal setting is a collegial activity undertaken by groups of staff. School and college aims are inevitably influenced by pressures from outside the organisation. The arguments about the National Curriculum in England and Wales are symptomatic of the diverse views about the extent and nature of prescription over the content of education. Institutions may be left with the task of interpreting external requirements rather than determining aims on the basis of their own assessment of student need (adapted from Bush, 1995, pp. 2–3).

Despite these difficulties, it is possible to set out certain general principles for the management of educational institutions. Everard and Morris (1990, pp. 11–12) state five such precepts for schools:

1. The raison d'être of a school is to promote its pupils' learning, within a curriculum acceptable to its stakeholders, or as prescribed by the law.
2. A school organization should meet these ends efficiently and cost-effectively.
3. In such an organization tensions will arise between professional autonomy and managerial control,

individuality and hierarchy, structural authority and participative decision-making, the head's dual roles of 'leading professional' and 'chief executive', the educational good of the many and the self-interest of the few, high principle and pragmatic expediency – and many other dilemmas that sometimes require a decision as to the lesser of two 'evils', e.g. being cruel in order to be kind.

4. Striking the correct balance in these dilemmas entails difficult judgements, which have to be referred to a set of values outside of and greater than those of the individuals in the organization.

5. At the highest level of abstraction, such values apply to, and often drive, all successful organizations, be they educational or commercial, and they act as bridges between the two.

Activity

Reflect on the discussion of aims and objectives set out above and explain the core purpose of your organisation. Please try to capture its essence in a single sentence.

❏ Comment

Your statement of purpose is likely to be a more specific version of the one-sentence definition given above. You may have modified the statement in one or more of the following ways:

1. By linking it to the age group or phase of education catered for by your school or college.

2. By relating it to the community served by the institution.

3. By broadening the term to include other aims as well as learning; these might involve social skills such as teamwork and good personal relationships.

The important point is that your purpose should be specific to the institution and its students and not simply be a repetition of statements of general purpose such as that given above.

The context of educational management

School and college management occurs in a specific social, economic and educational context. As social organisations, usually in the public sector, educational institutions are subject to legislative change as well as coping with rapid and multiple change arising from the wider society. The pace of educational change appears to have been accelerating in the 1980s and 1990s and there is little prospect of greater stability in the early years of the new millennium. Education is linked to the economy and all governments recognise that a skilled and educated workforce is a requirement for economic competitiveness:

> The pressure for developed and developing economies to become more efficient in order to compete effectively on the world stage has led to a heightened awareness of the links between educational capability and economic performance. A skilled workforce depends largely on the outputs of schools, colleges and universities. This has led to a plethora of legislation as governments have sought to raise educational standards (Bush, 1997, p. 5).

In England and Wales, and in many other countries, educational change has been characterised by simultaneous centralisation and decentralisation. Governments have sustained or tightened control of the curriculum, and its associated assessment and inspection, while giving schools and colleges greater control over resources, including budgets and staff management, within a framework of competition between institutions which has been described as a 'quasi-market' (Levačić, 1995).

Schools and colleges have to interpret and implement government imperatives but the greater challenge arises from the shift to self-management. The scope and nature of educational management in England and Wales changed dramatically with the implementation of the Education Reform Act 1988 (ERA). The ERA and subsequent legislation made fundamental changes to the previous pattern which had been established in 1944. Both central government and the schools gained powers while the main 'losers' were the local education authorities (LEAs) which could no longer exercise direct control over what were previously 'their' schools and colleges (Bush, 1995).

Caldwell and Spinks (1992) show that self-management is an international phenomenon; a 'mega-trend'. It is underpinned by the following assumptions:

1. Managers will be more responsive to their clients and communities if they are able to determine, to a greater extent than before, the nature and quality of education offered in their establishments.

2. Managers will be able to determine the precise mix of resources (teachers, support staff, materials, equipment) in order to achieve the school's specific objectives.

3. Staff will have the incentive to maximise efficiency in the use of resources because the ensuing savings will be available to the school or college to enhance educational quality further.

4. Standards will rise as clients, and parents as surrogate clients, articulate their requirements and schools respond to these needs or risk losing students to rival establishments.

Research evidence in England and Wales (Bush *et al.*, 1993; Levačić, 1995; Thomas and Martin, 1996) shows that heads generally welcome the greater flexibility and scope of self-management but it is too early to make a full assessment of its effectiveness. 'Autonomous schools and colleges may be regarded as potentially more efficient and effective but much depends on the nature and quality of internal management if the putative benefits of autonomy are to be realised' (Bush, 1995, p. 5).

International research evidence also tends to support the notion that autonomy is beneficial for schools and their students. Gaziel's (1998, pp. 329–30) research in Israel, for example, shows that devolution is perceived to increase autonomy in several important areas of school management:

> Those schools which were delegated greater powers in making internal decisions, which previously needed the Ministry of Education approvals, are perceived by school staff as having greater autonomy in making decisions with respect to internal school evaluation, institutional staff development, school curriculum design etc. than schools which had not been delegated the powers to do so.

A study of nine countries by the Organisation for Economic Co-operation and Development (OECD) gives a cautious welcome to self-management and concludes that it is likely to be beneficial:

> Greater autonomy in schools ...[leads] to greater effectiveness through greater flexibility in and therefore better use of resources; to professional development selected at school level; to more knowledgeable teachers and parents, so to better financial decisions; to whole school-planning and implementation with priorities set on the basis of data about student [outcomes] and needs (quoted in Thomas and Martin, 1996, p. 28).

The shift to self-management has placed schools and colleges in a competitive environment where success, or in certain circumstances their very survival, depends on their ability to meet client needs effectively. Educational institutions in many countries now match Carlson's (1975, p. 191) description of 'wild' organisations which 'do struggle for survival. Their existence is not guaranteed, and they do cease to exist. Support for them is closely tied to quality of performance, and a steady flow of clients is not assured. Wild organisations are not protected at vulnerable points as are domesticated organisations'.

This description is appropriate for self-managing institutions. The income of schools and colleges in England and Wales is tied to their success in recruiting students. While there are external judgements of quality through inspection, the ultimate test of success is recruitment rather than educational achievement.

Strategy and self-management

Self-management, in locating many powers at institutional level, provides the potential for a strategic approach. Because school and college leaders. and governing boards, are directly responsible for budgets, staffing and external relations, they are able to integrate these functions in a way which would have been impossible as recently as the 1980s:

> Because the levers of control are largely held at institutional level, it is both possible and desirable for leaders to adopt a strategic approach to management. This stance involves taking a holistic view of the organisation and planning for the long term within a framework of clearly articulated values and objectives. Strategic management requires the ability to integrate different aspects of the school to ensure the best possible educational outcomes. (Bush, 1998, p. vii).

◎ Reading

Please now read David Middlewood's 'Strategic management in education: an overview', Chapter 1 in Middlewood, D. and Lumby, J. (eds.) *Strategic Management in Schools and Colleges*. In doing so, please note his main points about:

1. **the relationship between strategy and self-management;**
2. **the differentiation of strategic thinking from operational management;**
3. **the nature of strategic management.**

❏ Comment

This chapter is wide ranging and you may have chosen to focus on many different issues. We have selected three aspects which seem to be particularly important for strategic management in education:

1. The need for a **proactive approach**. Because strategy is essentially long term, it requires a forward-looking stance with a clear vision of the future. If management is reactive, it is very difficult to adopt this longer-term perspective.

2. In his Table 1.1, Middlewood identifies several characteristics of strategic thinking and differentiates it from operational management. The main features are probably the following:

   a) a focus on the long-term;
   b) creativity;
   c) scanning the external environment; and
   d) adopting an overview; a 'helicopter' perspective.

3. The requirement for strategic managers to be accountable to stakeholders. These include the government agencies that fund schools and colleges, the students whose futures may depend on the quality of education they receive and the staff who must be well motivated if the organisation is to achieve its objectives.

❏ Building on key learning points

- Strategic management requires an overview of the organisation, which includes all its activities, and an extended timescale.
- Defining purpose is a central aspect of management and, in education, is expected to relate to learning.
- The creation of self-managing schools and colleges in many countries provides greater scope for leaders to adopt a strategic approach to management.

3. Vision, mission and strategy

This chapter considers:

- vision and vision-building;
- missions and mission statements; and
- the importance and limitations of strategic management.

Vision

A strategic approach to management requires an explicit sense of direction and purpose. Defining a clear vision for the organisation is an important stage in this process. The concept of vision has become increasingly important in the management of education, as Foreman (1998, p. 18) describes:

> Contemporary orthodoxy demands that leaders shall possess personal visions of a brighter future for themselves and their organisations, and will be able to communicate and demonstrate them with vigour, persuasiveness and conviction...Without vision, there can be no clear direction, no corporate way forward – and no commitment. Vision is the distinguishing feature of the leadership role.

Vision refers to a desirable future state of the organisation. It relates to the intended purposes of the school or college, expressed in terms of values and clarifying the direction to be taken by the institution. It should be inspirational so that organisational members are motivated to work towards it with pride and enthusiasm. It is closely identified with school improvement (Blum and Butler, 1989). The following definitions capture the essence of this concept:

> A mental image of a possible and desirable future state of the organisation...as vague as a dream or as precise as a goal or mission statement...a view of a realistic, credible, attractive future for the organisation, a condition that is better in some important ways than what now exists (Bennis and Nanus, 1985, p. 89).

> An image of what might be; an ideal which is unique to the person or the organisation and recognises dissatisfaction with the present. It is a catalyst for action, and reflects core values (Foreman, 1998, p. 22).

> A vision is a preferred future, a desirable state. It is an expression of optimism despite the bureaucratic surroundings or evidence to the contrary (Block, 1987, p. 103).

> The notion of 'vision' which is so popular nowadays, is more about the clarification and articulation of a set of values ...than a concrete image given by the head at the outset (Hopkins, 1996b, p. 35).

The 'popularity' of vision is evident in the work of the Teacher Training Agency (TTA) in England and Wales, notably in the National Standards for Headship and the associated training and assessment for the National Professional Qualification for Headship (NPQH). Heads are expected to 'provide' vision and to 'embody' that vision in their leadership of schools, to inspire pupils, staff, governors and parents.

The implication of the definitions presented above is that it should be specific to each school or college not simply a restatement of national values and priorities. The difficulty of developing such a specific vision should not be underestimated. Glatter and Weindling's (1993, pp. 19–20) discussion, drawing on Bolam et al.'s (1993) research on effective schools, takes a sceptical view of heads' claims that they have a vision for their schools:

All twelve heads said they had a vision, but in the majority of cases these lacked specific detail and tended to reflect the broad aims of British education...Few could be said to be genuinely inspiring...there was little evidence that teachers had played a significant part in shaping them...teachers generally were obliged to infer what the vision was about.

The generation and communication of a distinctive vision in schools and colleges are a deliberate process that needs a high priority if it is to be successful. We now turn to this process of vision-building.

❏ Vision-building

The concepts of leadership and vision are increasingly linked but Beare *et al.* (1993, p. 157) emphasise that the latter notion is not new despite its current prominence in the discourse of leadership and management:

The term 'vision' ... is not describing a new phenomenon in leadership. It is simply attaching a label to the sort of dream or constellation of goals or scenarios that form in the mind of everyone from time to time. What we now know is that these form readily in the minds of leaders who succeed in transforming their organisations.

Beare *et al.* (*ibid.*, p. 147) present ten 'emerging generalisations' for excellent leadership in schools. Three of these relate to the generation of vision:

- Outstanding leaders have a vision for their organisation.
- Vision must be communicated in a way which secures commitment among members of the organisation.
- Communication of vision requires communication of meaning.

The second of Beare *et al.*'s generalisations is arguably the key to the development of a shared vision. Fullan (1992, p. 121) emphasises the importance of vision-building but also demonstrates that it may be problematic: 'Vision-building...permeates the organisation with values, purpose and integrity for both the what and how of improvement...its formation, implementation, shaping, and reshaping in specific organisations is a constant process...While virtually everyone agrees that vision is crucial, the practice of vision-building is not well understood'.

Beare *et al.* (1993, pp. 156–7) offer several guidelines for the generation of vision:

- The vision of a school leader includes a mental image of a possible and desirable future state of the school.
- The vision will embody the leader's own view of what constitutes excellence in schooling.
- The vision of a school leader also includes a mental image of a possible and desirable future state for the broader educational scene and for society in general.
- The vision of a school leader also includes a mental image of a possible and desirable process of change through which the preferred future state will be achieved.
- Each aspect of the vision for a school reflects different assumptions, values and beliefs about such matters as the nature of humankind; the purpose of schooling; the roles of government, family and church in schooling; approaches to teaching and learning; and approaches to the management of change.
- There will be competing visions of schooling reflecting the many, often conflicting differences in assumptions, values and beliefs.

In seeking to build vision in schools and colleges, leaders should avoid a 'top-down' approach, forcing staff and stakeholders to embrace their ideas. Vision should enthuse staff, not make them resentful and unwilling participants in an imposed process. However, as Foreman (1998, p. 24) shows, this is not a straightforward development:

Vision cannot be imposed or mandated from above. Vision-building is about enrolling the interests and aspirations of others. But here lies the problem: the translation of personal dreams which animate and enthuse into something which enlists the support of others through appealing to their wants and values. For many, it is not a natural role.

Mission

'Mission' is another term which is often used to express the purpose of organisations. It is used to explain overall aims and philosophy and is often captured in a short sentence or passage. It is usually expected to be memorable and provide a guide to action for members of the organisation. While it is sometimes used interchangeably with 'vision', mission is usually regarded as a more specific expression of the values of the institution; a vehicle for translating the inspiration into reality. Everard and Morris (1990, p. 256) regard mission as 'fundamental': 'The starting point is a definition of the organisation's reason for being. Why does it exist? What is its central raison d'être or "core mission"?'

The mission is usually expressed in a statement or slogan but West-Burnham (1992, p. 71) says there may be disagreement about what is included in the statement, which has to serve several purposes. These may include:

- It characterises the school to its community.
- It provides a sense of direction and purpose.
- It serves as a criterion for policy-making.
- It sets the school culture.
- It generates consistency of action.
- It identifies clients.
- It serves to motivate and challenge.

The mission statement for Milton Keynes College in England incorporates several of these features, as its principal shows:

> The starting point for our strategic planning and management is the college's mission. Our mission defines purpose and embodies our educational philosophy and values. It is a reference point by which we make decisions, **determine** implementation strategies and policy, judge behaviour and evaluate our performance. It informs and guides our strategic direction (Limb, 1992, p. 168).

◉ Reading and Activity

Please now read the short section on 'Mission' (pp. 26–9) in Keith Foreman's 'Vision and mission in strategic management in schools and colleges', Chapter 2 in Middlewood, D. and Lumby, J. (eds.) *Strategic Management in Schools and Colleges.*

The author briefly considers the effectiveness of mission statements in both industry and education. Note the main features of mission and the criticisms that have been made of it.

Our comments appear below but please do not read them until you have completed the activity.

❑ Comment

This short passage is helpful in summarising the main features of mission. The notions of targeting, comparison with other organisations and internal change are useful dimensions of the concept. It also reinforces the relationship between mission and purpose.

The application of mission to education is shown to be problematic in the USA, Singapore and Britain. In the same chapter (p. 19), Foreman quotes Collins and Porras' (1991) strong criticisms of mission statements, which they say are 'terribly ineffective' and 'boring'. As mission statements are relatively new, the unanswered question is whether these weaknesses are inevitable or simply the product of a lack of experience in their preparation.

❏ Examples of mission statements

As we noted earlier, Everard and Morris (1990, p. 192) link mission to purpose but they point out that reaching agreement on the ingredients of mission tends to be more difficult. They suggest four alternative statements for a school. To:

1. educate children;
2. prepare children for life, citizenship and work;
3. be a lively centre for effective learning and development for the young; and
4. provide rewarding jobs for the staff teaching the children.

These points do not relate to a particular school and could be criticised as too general, a point made earlier about vision, which is supposed to be specific to one institution.

The difficulty of making mission statements specific to the individual school or college is illustrated by Stott and Walker's (1992) research in Singapore schools. They surveyed 20 heads of department in primary and secondary schools and concluded that their mission statements were rather similar:

> The uniqueness of each learning community was not being represented through their mission statements...Environmental factors point to need for schools to be different and to emphasise their distinctive competencies. In the mission-formulation process, therefore, there may be a need to consider how a school might effectively differentiate its provision (*ibid.*, p. 56).

Activity

Examine the four examples of mission statements given below and consider whether, and to what extent, they avoid the trap of being too general. Are they specific, do they provide a basis for action and are they memorable? Or are they 'boring' and 'ineffective' in line with Collins and Porras' (1991) criticism referred to earlier?

---

1. Wombwell High School, Barnsley, England

Wombwell High School will endeavour to create the opportunity for individuals to develop respect and responsibility through the provision of an appropriate curriculum, environment and relationships.

2. Caritas Francis Hsu College, Hong Kong

The mission of the College is to produce responsible and respectable graduates who are academically and professionally well educated and can fulfil the role of making contributions to the social and moral well-being of the community. Based on our belief in the value of the human person, the College is committed to providing study programmes for those who might have less opportunity of pursuing post-secondary education as well as those who wish to continue their personal and professional development at any stage of their lives.

3. Lebanese American University (Lebanon)

The Lebanese American University, which was founded by the Presbyterian Church (USA), is a multi-campus career-orientated university which shares the spiritual concerns of its founders in the search of God's Living Truth. Its objective is to serve the educational needs of Lebanon and the Middle East by being a community that is intellectually stimulating and responsive to the dynamics of its environment.

4. Hong Kong University of Science and Technology: Language Centre

The objectives of the language centre are:

To empower students by helping them:

- to study independently through English at university
- to work in the international setting of Hong Kong
- to communicate with the world beyond

To advance learning and knowledge through teaching and research, particularly in:

- innovative course development to meet students' needs
- innovative use of technology to develop learning materials
- excellence in teaching
- research relevant to language learners in Hong Kong
- local and international co-operation through publications and conferences
- making the Language Centre a fulfilling place to work and communicating that fulfilment to students

To assist in the economic and social development of Hong Kong by providing:

- relevant language services to students
- where resources permit, courses and expertise to university staff and other organisations in Hong Kong.

❏ Comment

Readers are likely to interpret these four mission statements in different ways. The Wombwell statement provides a worthwhile set of principles which might inform practice but they do not appear to be specific to the college. The Caritas, Francis Hsu and Lebanese American University (LAU) missions both have religious dimensions, and LAU also has a geographical element. In other respects, however, the statements are rather general although both are supported by more detailed objectives (not shown in this text). The Hong Kong University of Science and Technology statement is more precise, perhaps because it relates to a specific unit rather than the university as a whole, but lacks brevity. These four illustrate the difficulty of producing a mission statement which is short, memorable and specific. Has your institution succeeded on all three dimensions?

Strategy

Strategy is the third 'term' used to capture a sense of purpose and direction in organisations. As we noted earlier, it is distinguished by its holistic approach to management and by its extended timescale. It is also intended to be values-driven and to be linked to both vision and mission.

Until the shift to self-management in the late 1980s and 1990s, strategic management was the preserve of local, regional and national governments. They adopted an overview of the needs of education in their territories and developed plans to implement these ideas. These plans were typically expressed through the annual budget-setting process which allocated resources between categories of spending. Decisions were made about the relative priorities of different phases (preschool, primary, secondary, vocational education, etc.) as well as between different heads of expenditure (teachers, other staff, equipment, buildings, materials, etc.). These priorities were inevitably territory-wide and could not be linked to the specific needs of individual schools and colleges.

The implementation of the Education Reform Act, and its international equivalents, changed the focus of strategic management in many countries. While governments retained a budgetary role, they generally lost their control of the resource mix in individual schools and, in England and Wales, ceded all powers in respect of colleges which became independent of LEAs through incorporation.

The reduced capability of LEAs to plan strategically for their areas was regretted by some heads (Bullock and Thomas, 1997, p. 110) but most welcomed the freedom to manage their schools holistically and to integrate curriculum, finance, staff and external relations (Bush *et al.*, 1993; Levacic, 1995). Further education colleges experienced the most fundamental changes and Limb (1992, p. 170) shows the significance of incorporation to the adoption of a strategic approach at Milton Keynes College: 'The increased emphasis on strategic planning which resulted from the Education Reform Act, encouraged us to look more closely at the strategy element of planning.'

The links between self-management and strategic management are also evident in other countries. In Hong Kong, for example, the introduction of the School Management Initiative (SMI) in 1991 led to a focus on planning, as Wong *et al.* (1998, p. 67) suggest:

> The School Management Initiative... is a major restructuring of the operations of secondary and primary schools, with the belief that greater self-management can enhance school performance... An official aim of the SMI scheme is 'to encourage more systematic planning and evaluation of programmes of activities in schools and reporting their performance' (Education Department, Hong Kong, 1993). Consequently, the development of an annual school plan is one of the changes required under SMI... With self-management, schools are more free to address their own problems and, in order to manage changes and routines in a controlled manner, systematic and effective planning is important and highly desirable.

Caldwell and Spinks (1992, p. 92) make it clear that strategy is a key component of the principal's role, which is exercised by:

- keeping abreast of trends and issues, threats and opportunities;
- discerning megatrends;
- sharing their knowledge;
- establishing structures and processes which enable the school to set priorities and formulate strategies;
- ensuring that the attention of the school community is focused on matters of strategic importance;
- monitoring the implementation of strategies as well as emerging strategic issues; facilitating an ongoing process of review.

West-Burnham (1994b, p. 84) defines strategic planning as:

> A process operating in an extended time-frame (three to five years) which translates vision and values into significant, measurable and practical outcomes. Although the primary responsibility of senior management, the process requires two-way communication at all stages and has to be focused on the core purpose and practical activities of the school or college.

Caldwell and Spinks (1988, p. 61), who have played an important role in disseminating self-management practice, adopt a similar definition in their discussion of 'corporate planning':

> A continuous process in administration which links goal-setting, policy-making, short-term and long-term planning, budgeting and evaluation in a manner which spans all levels of the organisation, secures appropriate involvement of people according to their responsibility for implementing plans as well as of people with an interest or stake in the outcomes of those plans, and provides a framework for the annual planning, budgeting and evaluation cycle.

However, in researching the process of strategic planning in further education, Lumby (1999, p. 75) identifies the importance of the process itself: 'All of the principals referred to the unimportance of the strategic planning document and the importance of the process.' What appeared to be important for them about this process was the articulation of the 'values and understandings' that was involved: 'This may involve a limited group, such as the senior management team, or the entire college community, but it is essentially a conversation, an exchange which is only secondarily designed to delineate action. Primarily, it is an act of union, designed to reinforce commitments and motivation' (*ibid.*)

❏ Limitations of strategic management

Despite the difficulties of practicalities, strategic planning is essentially seen as a rational approach to organisational management. It assumes that leaders can acquire a measure of control over the often turbulent, and always changing, external environment. Strategy is seductive; it appears to offer the potential to help managers to create order from chaos, to gain mastery over external forces, to integrate often disparate processes and to look beyond the immediate problems to a brighter future. In practice, though, there are several limitations, as West-Burnham (1994b, pp. 87–8) suggests:

> However attractive this model may appear in terms of coherence and relative simplicity it is not unproblematic. Any rational approach to planning will inevitably be compromised by a number of factors.
>
> 1. The extent to which vision and values are shared – cultural homogeneity is an aspiration rather than the norm in most educational institutions
> 2. The problems in identifying a vision which is capable of changing to meet the perceptions and legitimate demands of all stakeholders over a significant time-scale
> 3. The concern that the dominance of one vision can over-simplify reality and thereby inhibit creativity, i.e. the organization becomes mechanistic.

Some of these problems are illustrated by Wallace's (1991) research on strategic planning in two primary and two secondary schools in England. He chronicles a series of unforeseen events which disrupted planning in his case-study schools: 'While some plans were carried through as predicted, the substance of schools' development plans became less representative of changing priorities, targets and detailed plans as the year progressed and did not in practice guide ongoing development planning' (*ibid.*, p. 154).

Wallace (*ibid.*) summarises the factors which disrupted strategic planning at these schools, including the following:

- The multiplicity of goals, some of which came and went, that competed for the attention at any time.
- Unpredictable crises and issues affecting innovations and other work, alongside the predictability of most routine activity in school.
- The inability to predict some shifts in central government and LEA policies while being able to predict the possibility if not the timing, of others.
- The combination of relative uncertainty about some external innovations or the arrangements for their introduction and clarity about others.

These factors illustrate the desirability of strategic planning being undertaken in a stable context. In practice, the rapid pace of change means that strategy is an ongoing, evolving and uncertain process. Rational models underpin much of the normative literature on school and college management, including that emanating from government agencies. Glover *et al.* (1996, p. 136) identify the Office for Standards in Education (Ofsted) model as being 'highly rational and technicist... Educational objectives need to be explicitly defined and selected and then implemented through action plans ... The model can be seen as approaching the educational equivalent of formal strategic planning'.

Wong *et al.* (1998, p. 69) argue that 'purely rational approaches to planning may not be appropriate'. Referring to the Hong Kong context they advocate a process of flexible planning and the participation of teachers in the planning process, an approach consistent with the collegial model which we shall examine in chapter 5. They conclude that participative and flexible planning is more likely to be effective than traditional planning models:

> For planning to be effective in co-ordinating school activities and producing positive outcomes, self-managing schools in Hong Kong should adopt a flexible planning approach... In this model, responding to the environment is a key concept... Teachers should be encouraged and helped to participate in planning decisions. If the plan is developed collaboratively, teachers' professional knowledge and experience are utilised and there should be better scanning and evaluation of the environment' (*ibid.*, pp. 77–8).

However, the size of the organisation may be problematic in achieving the full participation of staff. One of the college principals interviewed in Lumby's (1999, p. 76) research asked:

How do you get an organisation of 400 people who are all working in different ways, in different sets of people within the organisation, and don't appreciate each others' culture and values, to own something that is called a strategic plan? That is what all the models say you are supposed to do.

◉ Reading

Further discussion of vision, mission and strategy may be found in the following chapters from EMDU course texts: Foreman, K. (1998) 'Vision and mission', in Middlewood, D. and Lumby, J. (eds.) *Strategic Management in Schools and Colleges*, London, Paul Chapman Publishing; West-Burnham, J. (1994) 'Strategy policy and planning', in Bush, T. and West-Burnham, J. (eds.) *The Principles of Educational Management*, Harlow, Longman.

❏ Building on key learning points

- Strategic management requires a vision of the organisation to provide an explicit sense of direction and purpose.
- Vision is an important quality for educational leaders.
- Mission statements are often produced by schools and colleges but they are often not memorable and specific to the organisation.
- Strategic planning is based on a rational management model but this underestimates its problematic aspects, including its lack of flexibility in responding to unforeseen events.

---

4. Leadership in educational management

This chapter considers:

- the distinction between leadership and management;
- different types and aspects of leadership;
- gender and leadership; and
- leadership roles.

Introduction

The concept of leadership is complex and evolving. Most of what is written about leadership draws on western culture, particularly that of North America. However, leadership is likely to be viewed differently in different cultures: 'there remains much to learn about cultural understandings of leadership. Administrative textbooks rarely touch upon the expectations that culture creates for leaders' (Bryant, 1998, p. 7).

Hofstede (1980; 1991) has conducted extensive research on the relative importance of the following variables in a range of cultures:

1. *Individualism*, individual autonomy versus responsibility to the group.
2. *Masculinity*, how far roles in society are differentiated between men and women.
3. *Power distance*, the extent to which inequality is accepted.
4. *Uncertainty avoidance*, the level of concern about law and order.

Consideration of these variables (Dimmock, 1998) show how they may be relevant to the ways that leadership is viewed in different societies. For example, out of a total of 53 countries, the USA, Australia and Britain are ranked first, second and third at the individualistic end of the spectrum, whilst Hong Kong, Singapore, Malaysia and Thailand are towards the collectivist end, thus placing greater importance on the needs of the group as opposed to the individual. Similarly, the power distance relationship shows a sharp divide between the western and eastern countries with collectivist societies having a high power-distance index and individualistic societies having low power-distance ratings. However, there is little difference in terms of masculinity/femininity and uncertainty avoidance between any of the seven countries named above. Bjerke and Al-Meer (1993, p. 34) applied the research instruments of Hofstede to Saudi Arabian managers and concluded that they:

> tend to have a high uncertainty avoidance orientation. For example, Saudi managers, as Moslems and Arabs, do not tolerate persons who deviate from Islamic teachings and Arab traditions. They are very loyal to their organisations. Also, they do not like conflict. However, if they are forced, they resolve disagreements by authoritarian behaviour.

The differences between eastern and western countries in the way that inequalities in power, the importance of the individual, the nature of gender roles and tolerance of uncertainty are regarded are of importance in understanding how the role of the leader may be perceived differently in different cultures.

Harber and Davies (1997) make a strong claim that leadership in education in developing countries, specifically African countries, tends towards the authoritarian. They put forward several hypotheses to back up their claim:

> classroom teaching tends to be authoritarian in style and since headteachers are recruited from the ranks of classroom teachers without further training they are likely to maintain the same style;

> the education systems tend to be highly centralised and 'top-down';

> there are traditional notions of masculine leadership style: 'with strength, hierarchy and dominance being the paramount managerial model' (adapted from *ibid.*, pp. 60–1).

Bryant (1998, p. 18), having undertaken qualitative research with Native Americans, illustrates how western concepts of leadership should not be taken for granted:

> Native American culture can be unsettling. Simple values that we take for granted are sometimes turned upside down. Nepotism is a good example. In western culture, ... the notion of doing things that benefit family and relatives is seen as unethical. In some places there are laws forbidding nepotism. Yet in Native American cultures, taking care of family and relatives is one of the first obligations of a leader. Nepotism becomes a positive value.

Activity

In pursuing ideas relating to leadership we now inevitably draw on a range of mainly western material. However, as you read the following sections, it may be useful to question the extent to which the concepts actually apply to leadership in your school or college.

In Chapter 2 we stated that the distinction between leadership and management may be overdrawn, and that both contribute to effectiveness in education. In practice, leadership and management functions are likely to overlap and to be carried out within the same role.

However, in analysing leadership it may be helpful to give further consideration to how the concepts differ.

Leadership and management

As stated earlier, leadership tends to be equated with vision and values and management to processes and structures:

> Leadership and management are not synonymous terms. One can be a leader without being a manager. One can, for example, fulfil many of the symbolic, inspirational, educational and normative functions of a leader and thus represent what an organization stands for without carrying any of the formal burdens of management. Conversely, one can manage without leading. An individual can monitor and control organizational activities, make decisions, and allocate resources without fulfilling the symbolic, normative, inspirational, or educational functions of leadership (Schon, 1984, p. 36).

Here the differentiation is not intended to distinguish between roles. Schon goes on to say that since we generally expect managers to lead, it may be permissible to treat management and leadership as one, although he does identify the concepts of management as science and the art of managing. This latter concept may have more in common with leadership.

❏ The 'art' of leadership
The art may mean intuitive judgement and skill, 'knowing in practice', but it may also indicate

'reflection in action'. Schon (*ibid.*, p. 42) designates this as: 'reflection, in a context of action, on phenomena which are perceived as incongruent with intuitive understandings.' Or, 'a reflective conversation with the situation.'

In addition the reflecting in action of the manager/leader is done in the context of the culture of an organisation which acts as a store of past experience, organisations being 'repositories of cumulatively built-up knowledge'. Organisations and their culture may be more or less conducive to learning and change and this will affect the scope and direction of the manager's reflection in action.

❑ Tactical and strategic management

The division between management and leadership may be akin to the division into *tactical* and *strategic* leadership identified by Sergiovanni (1984a, p. 105): 'Tactical leadership involves analyses which lead to administrative action and means of minor magnitude, which are of small scale, and which serve larger purposes. Strategic leadership, by contrast, is the art and science of enlisting support for broader policies and purposes and for devising longer-range plans.'

Sergiovanni identifies the strategic with beliefs and commitment. He identifies the tactical skill necessary for a situational approach to leadership – 'careful reading of situations and applying the right doses of the correct mix of leadership styles' – and contrasts it with:

> a leader who has certain purposes, beliefs, and commitment to what the school or university is and can be and who can communicate these in a fashion which rallies others to the cause . . . What a leader stands for is more important than what he or she does. The meanings a leader communicates to others is more important than his or her specific leadership style (*ibid.*, p. 106).

❑ 'Higher-order' leadership

Whilst managers may be expected to exhibit leadership most theorists do draw a distinction between 'higher order' leadership and more run-of-the-mill management. Bennis (1984) deduced that the Chief Executive Officers (CEOs) of organisations he studied identified themselves as leaders.

They were concerned with: 'their organisation's basic purposes, why it exists and its general direction . . . they were concerned not with "doing things right" (the overriding concern of managers) but with "doing the right thing"'(*ibid.*, p. 66).

❑ Leadership 'forces'

Elsewhere, Sergiovanni (1984b) identifies five leadership 'forces', which he regards as hierarchical. The first, the technical 'force' (management), underpins the others, but the top of the pyramid, and the most advanced of the 'forces' are the normative aspects of leadership concerned with values and culture:

- *Technical* – management techniques. The leader as 'management engineer'.
- *Human* – social and interpersonal resources. The leader as 'human engineer'.
- *Educational* – expert knowledge about education. The leader as 'clinical practitioner'.
- *Symbolic* – focusing attention on what is important. The leader as 'chief'.
- *Cultural* – building a unique school culture. The leader as 'high priest'.

This brief consideration of the nature of leadership and management indicates that leaders in schools and colleges are charged with a range of responsibilities that have enormous implications for the well-being and improvement of the institution. In particular, leaders are associated with the development and communication of a vision for the school or college (see Chapter 3). The communication of that vision implies much about the nature of leadership today, for it is expected that the leader(s) will be able to encourage the involvement and understanding of staff. The level of importance and responsibilities of leadership are also emphasised by the links that are made between school effectiveness and improvement and the quality of leadership: 'the purposeful leadership of the staff by the headteacher' (Mortimore *et al.*, 1988, p. 118) is the first of the list of factors associated with effective schools.

Theory and practice

The differentiation that is made between leadership and management may disguise the fact that many leaders in education actually spend a large proportion of their time in tasks that could best be termed administrative or even clerical. Torrington and Weightman (1989) observed senior staff working in English schools and found that a substantial proportion of their time was spent on administration (defined as work that could be done by an intelligent 16-year-old) and on the technical aspects of the job, such as classroom teaching. This would appear to leave little time for the areas of work defined as leading or managing.

A review of what headteachers actually do, undertaken by Fullan (1991, p. 146), found consistently that:

> Virtually all the time of headteachers is taken up with one-to-one personal encounters, meetings and telephone calls.

> Headteachers' workdays were sporadic and characterized simultaneously by brevity, variety and fragmentation.

> Headteachers perform on average 149 tasks a day with constant interruptions – in one study 59 per cent of their observed activities were interrupted.

> Most of their activities (84 per cent) were brief (one to four minutes).

> Headteachers demonstrated a tendency to engage themselves in the most current and pressing situation. They invested little time in reflective planning.

> Most of their time is spent on administrative housekeeping matters, maintaining order and crisis management.

Although there is little written on what leaders do in schools and colleges in areas other than North America and Europe, one study of primary heads in Barbados (Sealy, 1992, quoted in Harber and Davies, 1997) showed that the pattern there was little different from that indicated above. The heads engaged in very many different activities in the day, so that the longest single activity was likely to be having lunch. Paperwork and correspondence took up a large proportion of their time.

Although 'the job of headteacher is . . . messy, fragmented, untidy and event-driven' (Harber and Davies, 1997, p. 65), headteachers and other leaders in education do aspire to lead in a way that may transcend the day-to-day reality.

 Reading

It is suggested that you now read the chapter 'Leadership in educational management' by Marianne Coleman, Chapter 3 in Bush, T. and West-Burnham, J. (eds.) *The Principles of Educational Management*. This chapter will provide you with an overview of the basic styles of leadership, of the concept of leadership in organisational theory and of the aspects of leadership that appear to be particularly relevant to an educational environment. Many of these aspects will be developed in the following sections.

❑ Comment

You will have seen from this chapter that there are two underlying ways of analysing styles of leadership: one is on the range from autocratic to democratic, and is associated with the work of Tannenbaum and Schmidt (1973); the other is that based on the relative dominance in a leader of 'concern for people and relationships' or 'concern for production or results'; this theory is associated with Blake and Mouton (1964). These concepts are useful in examining leadership in organisational theory where an emphasis is placed on the situational or contingency theories which recognise the interaction of leaders and their environments: 'They allow for the fact that appropriate and successful leadership style and behaviour will vary in different situations' (Coleman, 1994a, p. 59).

It may be the case that different leadership styles suit different groups in differing situations, for example, the leadership style that might be most appropriate to a school identified by the inspectorate as 'failing' might be very different from that which would suit a school that has been identified as 'moving' (Hopkins, 1994b). The leadership style appropriate to a well integrated primary school with eight teachers is likely to be different from that found in a well managed college employing hundreds of lecturers divided between four faculties, providing education for the range of adult learners. However, there may be some dimensions of good leadership that are, in principle, common to leadership in an educational environment. Amongst these are: the importance of vision; the benefits of transformational leadership; placing the education of pupils and students at the forefront of planning and management; and the moral or ethical dimension of leadership in education. In addition, leadership in education has been challenged by the increasing autonomy of schools and colleges in some countries, placing new and different responsibilities on educational leaders, particularly in relation to their ability to handle strategic issues. A further dimension of leadership that may be applicable to leadership of all educational institutions is that of gender, particularly as qualities of leadership are generally identified with the male (Schein, 1994).

The following list of generalisations, drawn from a review of the literature on leadership in education (Beare *et al.*, 1989a; 1993), reflects a concern with the areas outlined above. You will be asked to return to this list later as you reflect on current thinking on the nature of leadership in educational management. Reference has already been made to some of these generalisations in connection with the concept of vision (see p. 11).

1. Emphasis should be given to transformational rather than transactional leadership.
2. Outstanding leaders have a vision for their organisation.
3. Vision must be communicated in a way which secures commitment among members of the organisation.
4. Communication of vision requires communication of meaning.
5. Issues of value – 'what ought to be' – are central to leadership.
6. The leader has an important role in developing culture of organisation.
7. Studies of outstanding schools provide strong support for school-based management and collaborative decision-making.
8. There are many kinds of leadership forces – technical, human, educational, symbolic and these should be widely dispersed throughout the school.
9. Attention should be given to institutionalising vision if leadership of the transforming kind is to be successful.
10. Both 'masculine' and 'feminine' stereotype qualities are important in leadership, regardless of the gender of the leader (Beare *et al.*, 1989a, p. 108; 1993, p. 147).

Transformational and transactional leadership

The principal who practises transformational leadership is not relying only on his or her personal charisma, but is attempting to empower staff and share leadership functions. Transformational leadership may be contrasted with transactional leadership which: 'is based on an exchange of services (from a teacher, for example) for various kinds of rewards (salary recognition, and intrinsic rewards) that the leader controls, at least in part' (Leithwood, 1992, p. 69).

However, Bass and Avolio (1994) offer a two-factor theory of leadership where transformational leadership may exist alongside transactional leadership, which is seen to be central in maintaining the organisation and ensuring that the normal course of events run smoothly.

Transformational leadership is specifically linked with the notion of improvement. Bass and Avolio (*ibid.*, p. 2) state that transformational leadership is seen when leaders:

stimulate interest among colleagues and followers to view their work from new perspectives,

generate awareness of the mission or vision of the team and organization,

develop colleagues and followers to higher levels of ability and potential, and

motivate colleagues and followers to look beyond their own interests toward those that will benefit the group.

Alternatively, they refer to transformational leadership as the four i's:

1. *Idealised influence* (leaders are seen as role models for others).
2. *Inspirational motivation*.
3. *Intellectual stimulation*.
4. *Individualised consideration* (including leaders acting as coach or mentor to individuals in the institution).

As indicated above, leadership is situational, i.e. leaders may exhibit different styles and aspects of leadership depending on the specific context within which they are operating. However, those leaders who display what is termed 'an optimal leadership profile' exhibit transformational leadership and back up their transactional leadership with positive reinforcement and reward rather than correction. Bass and Avolio (*ibid.*, pp. 5–6) state that:

Many research studies have been completed in business and industry, government, the military, educational institutions, and non-profit organizations, all of them showing that transformational leaders, ... were more effective and satisfying as leaders than transactional leaders, although the best of leaders frequently do some of the latter but more of the former.

Studies in educational institutions have indicated that transformational leaders appear to be:

in continuous pursuit of three fundamental goals:

1) helping staff members develop and maintain a collaborative, professional school culture;
2) fostering teacher development; and
3) helping them solve problems together more effectively (Leithwood, 1992, pp. 69–70).

However, practice may differ considerably from this idealised state of affairs. Research on professional development to support educational changes in Hong Kong found that: 'The administrators involved in the study saw a very limited place for teachers in planning professional development. They suggested strongly that planning for professional development was the responsibility of the principal and other executive members ... Very few respondents indicated any active role for teachers in planning professional development' (Walker and Cheng, 1996, p. 206).

Burns (1978) is credited with first identifying transformational leadership. He does not endorse the two-factor theory of leadership, but rather considers transformational leadership to be at the opposite end of the spectrum from transactional leadership. This represents a very different view of transformational leadership to the two-factor theory of leadership, where transformational and transactional leadership may be identified in a single person (Bass and Avolio, 1994). A study of eight research projects from Singapore, Australia, Canada and the USA investigating the two-factor theory of leadership showed some support for both its internal and external validity (Leithwood *et al.*, 1996, p. 828). For example, qualitative evidence collected from 51 Texas school superintendents showed that: 'they believed transactional practices to be necessary and associated them with routine management, whereas transformational practices were associated with their change efforts' (*ibid.*, p. 820).

Research on transformational leadership has also been analysed with regard to the effects of this type of leadership. Some of the findings from an analysis of 20 studies on transformational leadership appear to indicate that:

Transformational leadership, as a whole, is strongly related to satisfaction with the leader and positive perceptions of the leader's effectiveness.

Transformational leadership, as a whole, is strongly related to the willingness of organizational members to engage in extra effort.

Organization level effects, such as teachers' perceptions of effectiveness and improvement, are positively associated with transformational leadership.

The leadership qualities associated with transformational effects are: charisma/vision/inspiration, intellectual stimulation, and individualised consideration (adapted from *ibid.*, pp. 828–9).

Although the conclusions are drawn from a wide range of studies, both quantitative and qualitative, Leithwood *et al.* (*ibid.*) note that there are positive effects associated with several identified forms of leadership in education. Amongst these is educational or educative leadership, also known as 'instructional leadership' in the USA.

Educational leadership

Throughout the literature relating to leadership in education, the theme of the central importance of education, or of teaching and learning, recurs. However, current practice in the UK in colleges of further education is for leadership to tend to lie with individuals who have specialisms in areas such as finance and human resource management, rather than being educationalists *per se*. Nevertheless, current research on school effectiveness stresses the importance of what goes on in the classroom and educational leadership is seen to be about providing a culture within which teaching and learning will prosper:

We presume that the quality of school life is greatly dependent on the quality of students' experience in the classroom. It follows that educative leadership will be central to the negotiations of what is to be regarded as valuable in the curriculum and what is believed to be excellent in teaching methods. This approach to leadership will nurture and protect these ideas of exemplary practice. To achieve this condition means defining excellence in specific terms. It also means planning in sophisticated ways to achieve desired outcomes. Educative leaders should, therefore, take responsible leadership actions to create organisational cultures that enhance the growth and development of all involved in teaching and learning (Duignan and Macpherson, 1992, p. 83).

The key quality linking leadership to effective schools in a large-scale study in Israel was found to be the ability to determine clear organisational goals towards which teachers could work: 'Effective school principals do not only spend their time on explicit internal controls, such as monitoring instruction, but rather stress goal emphasis and goal consensus mechanisms to direct teachers' attentions to specific activities through developing a clear understanding of their contribution to the total organizational output' (Goldring and Pasternak, 1994, p. 251).

The qualities identified by Duignan and Macpherson as applying to educative leaders are, in many ways, similar to those identified with transformational leaders. The stress is on encouraging and empowering those directly responsible for face-to-face teaching. Thus the educative leader:

1. Creates opportunities to allow participants in any change process to reflect on their practice and to develop personal understandings of the nature and implications of the change for themselves;
2. Encourages those involved in the implementation of an improvement to form social groups to provide for mutual support during the change process;
3. Provides opportunities for positive feedback for all involved in the change; and
4. Must be sensitive to the possible outcomes of any development process and provide the conditions necessary for feedback and follow-up so that those involved have the opportunity to discuss and rethink their ideas and practice (Duignan and Macpherson, 1992, p. 84).

The practical implications for leadership are clear. The principal should ensure there is a stress on professional development related to reflection on classroom practice and developed within a culture of collaboration. In addition, Fidler (1997, p. 32) notes the practical implications for instructional leadership as including:

managing the curriculum and teaching, including the organisation of pupil grouping and time allocation, but also stimulating curriculum development;

supervising teaching;

monitoring student progress; and

providing a positive teaching climate.

However, in summing up the research that has been undertaken on educative leadership, Northfield (1992, p. 100) stresses: 'For the principal, as for any educative leader, the key features are the leader (as a learner) providing opportunities for participants to develop personal understanding and encouraging the conditions for reflection in practice.'

This idea of the central importance of learning is taken up by Sergiovanni (1998), who refers to pedagogical leadership in terms of it adding value by the development of social, academic and intellectual capital in students and teachers. The term capital is not used in its strictly economic sense, but in terms of adding value to both student and teacher learning: 'Instead of increasing material value, pedagogical leadership adds value by developing various forms of human capital' (*ibid.*, p. 38).

The moral and ethical dimension of leadership

Leadership in schools carries a particular onus; heads and principals are acting *in loco parentis*, and therefore bear the responsibility for the experiences of the students in the school. It is perhaps the nature of this responsibility that identifies educational leadership as different in kind from other types of leadership, although West-Burnham (1994c, p. 26) does point out that the type of management that is unsuitable for children may be regarded as: 'equally inappropriate for adults'. Hodgkinson (1991, pp. 62–3) also draws attention to the difficulty of identifying goals in education as opposed to any other organisation. However, in this he also identifies a strength relating to the values to be endorsed:

these very difficulties are the source of peculiar leadership opportunities: the opportunity to discover, clarify and defend the ends of education, to motive towards those ends; the opportunity to discover means and invent process ... and the opportunity to create and establish morally grounded evaluation and legitimate it for all the participants in the great co-operative educational project. All of which means that educational leadership is especially difficult, especially challenging and especially moral.

Bottery (1992, p. 190) makes a strong normative case for the rejection of the historically based paternalistic style of leadership and endorses a leadership style which encourages a democratic, participative culture:

democratic heads will want to involve staff and pupils in the school's running, not to produce better results and have a happier staff and pupils, but to educate the school's members in their rights and responsibilities as citizens. They will want to provide opportunities for others to discuss matters of policy and implementation, not to ensure that prior preparation avoids confrontation and opposition, nor even to ensure that all knowledge is pooled to produce better results, but rather to provide school members with the opportunity to develop themselves and their community.

Sergiovanni (1998, p. 43) goes further to claim: 'The source of authority for leadership is found neither in bureaucratic rules and procedures nor in personalities and styles of leaders but in shared values, ideas and commitments.'

These values of educational leadership are also endorsed in respect of developing countries, where there tends to be a bureaucratic style of management, and an authoritarian style of leadership sometimes as a result of the inheritance of colonialism (Harber and Davies, 1997). It is claimed that democratic values, including participation and transparency, are likely to increase school effectiveness:

> This is because, while these values in themselves do not provide 'answers' for developing countries in the same way that Western management techniques often purport to do, they both allow for the free discussion among key participants of a possible range of locally relevant answers and, in educating for a democratic political system, encourage a macro-political context where such free and peaceful debate is possible (*ibid*, p. 151).

Within a basically democratic context, there may still be ethical dilemmas for educational leaders. Grace (1995, pp. 146–7) illustrates the moral, ethical and professional dilemmas of educational leaders with examples of the conflict felt by headteachers between their desire to co-operate with other schools and the pressure to compete with those schools engendered by recent reforms in England and Wales:

> In the ideological and value struggles between professional community and autonomous advantage, the participants were, in the main, remaining loyal to an existing culture which emphasized the former. For some, the enhanced autonomy of local management of schools was a sufficient indicator of 'progress', without the need for the destruction of local education networks.

Their increased financial autonomy brought them other ethical dilemmas concerned with teacher employment, particularly where the need to reduce expenditure led to taking decisions about redundancy.

Leadership of the autonomous school or college

Although leadership of the autonomous school or college may have provided a range of dilemmas, the changes have also brought about challenges and opportunities for leadership, not least of which is the possibility of the increase in efficiency and effectiveness of autonomous institutions. Caldwell and Spinks (1992, p. 57), considering leadership in autonomous schools, emphasise the importance of educational leadership and state that: 'in the final analysis, the case for self-management must be based on benefits for students in terms of gains in learning outcomes.'

Marsh D. (1992, p. 16) lists the increased responsibilities of a college and links the increase to the likelihood that leadership will tend towards a transformational, empowering model. The responsibilities include:

- do its own recruiting, hiring, personnel evaluation and firing;
- continuously acquire new skills and train its staff;
- formulate and track its own budgets;
- make capital investment as needed;
- constantly monitor and control its quality standards (or those of BS5750), inspection and trouble-shooting;

- suggest and develop new products and businesses;
- work on the improvement of everything all the time;
- develop and ensure its own detailed standards for productivity, quality and improvement and make them tough;
- be student centred and 'upside-down' from the orientation of the 80s.

The range involved leads to the conclusion that such a college 'cannot be run by command', but by 'persuasion and consent' (*ibid.*).

One of the aspects of leadership that has developed as a result of the increase in autonomy of educational institutions in certain countries is the importance of representing the school or college to the larger community and of acting as a potential gate-keeper between the institution and the wider world. Principals of the trial South African Model C schools, which were given greater control of their finances than other schools, identified marketing as one of the major changes to their role (Steyn and Squelch, 1994).

Beare *et al.* (1989a, p. 235) identify three fundamental aspects of the relationship between schools and the community in which they function:

1. Image has a powerful impact on how well the child learns, because the parents' attitudes to the school have a direct impact on the child.
2. A large number of teachers do not seem to appreciate that the school is only one element in a much larger educational enterprise.
3. Image begets public esteem; esteem creates public support.

There appears to be an overwhelming consensus that the management of external relations is a fundamental concern of leadership, linked as it is to outcomes, relationships and esteem. Caldwell and Spinks (1992, p. 156–7) make this relationship quite explicit, arguing for responsive leadership with the following components:

1. Commitment to the notion that the school is an institution which has been established to serve the interests of society as a whole, and the community in which it is situated.
2. Recognizing that those whose interests are served are entitled to have information to enable judgements to be made about the extent to which the school is addressing and achieving expectations.
3. Nurturing a culture which values critical reflection.
4. Identifying valid and reliable indicators for use in accountability.
5. Analysing and validating information derived from evaluation and review and working with others to refine overall management strategy and decision-making in the annual management cycle.

Foskett (1998) identifies the importance of one aspect of external relations, that of marketing to both schools and colleges, although the degree of importance and type of approach may vary according to the phase of education. For FE colleges, marketing 'has become a major preoccupation . . . in the period since incorporation (post 1992)' (*ibid.*, p. 54). However, he considers that for primary schools, the selling aspect of marketing is relatively unimportant, with the emphasis being on relationships and the importance of word-of-mouth promotion. In secondary schools, the marketing emphasis tends to relate to parental choice.

Marketing is an important aspect of external relations which has specific applicability to strategic management, and one where the headteacher or principal has consistently taken the lead role in schools, although there is now evidence (*ibid.*) that the responsibility is being shared with the senior management team (SMT), or an advisory body whose membership is wider than the SMT.

Strategic leadership

Identifying a strategy that may include a marketing orientation is increasingly important in colleges and most schools. The central role the principal and SMT play exemplifies the importance of leadership in strategic management. *The National Standards for Headteachers* (TTA, 1998, p. 9) identify 'strategic direction and development of the school' as the first of the key areas of headship, defining this as: 'Headteachers working with the governing body, develop a strategic view for the school in its community and analyse and plan for its future needs and further development within the local, national and international context.'

In relation to strategic planning in further education, Lumby (1998, p. 102) comments on the importance of the leadership role: 'Achieving any goal depends on more than clarity. The power base and capability of the person responsible underpin the capacity to achieve change.'

Stress has already been placed on the role of the leader in establishing a vision for the school or college. However, leadership also relates to strategy implementation:

> It is not enough for leaders to have the vision, sell it and then move on, leaving others to translate it into action. Implementation of the strategic plan needs continual monitoring and evaluation by those with the creative ability to understand where diversions may be appropriate and how obstacles can be surmounted. Strategic plans should be, after all, liberating and not constraining (Hall, 1998, p. 145).

◎ Reading and **Activity**

Please now read Valerie Hall's chapter, 'Strategic leadership in education: becoming, being, doing', Chapter 10 in Middlewood, D. and Lumby, J. (eds.) *Strategic Management in Schools and Colleges*.

In reading, please note the references to areas we have already considered, such as:

- the relationship between management and leadership;
- vision;
- transformational leadership;
- educational leadership;
- moral and ethical leadership; and
- leadership in the autonomous school or college.

There are also references to the links between strategic leadership and the concepts of school improvement and school effectiveness, which will be considered in Chapter 6.

❏ Comment

An important point made by Hall (1998, p. 134) is the tension between identifying leaders as principals and SMTs whilst also advocating a collaborative culture and the sharing of leadership functions. A further aspect of strategic leadership considered in the chapter is the relative importance of structures, particularly the use of teams. A related aspect of strategic management is the importance of managing people. Hall stresses that this may be most successful where the leadership style of the principal is empowering rather than emphasising 'power over'.

Two qualities of strategic leadership that emerge from the reading and elsewhere are the need for leaders to be flexible to cope with the unexpected, and the related need for them to have 'helicopter vision', that is, the ability to take the broad view. West-Burnham (1997, p. 243) calls for a reconceptualisation of leadership to allow schools to change to: 'respond to a changing world'. He stresses (adapted from *ibid.* pp. 235–43) the need for:

intellectualism to strengthen the educative role and reflection;

artistry – relating leadership to vision, creativity and communication;

spirituality – principles or 'higher order perspectives';

moral confidence or integrity of values;

subsidiarity or the 'willing surrendering of power' as opposed to the delegation of power;

emotional intelligence, the ability to know yourself and others and handle interpersonal relations.

This reconceptualisation uses a new vocabulary in relation to leadership but stresses many of the same themes of vision, ethical leadership and empowerment. However, the use of different language encourages a change of mind-set in relation to leadership. A change in mind-set with regard to leadership may also occur through using the concept of gender in the analysis of leadership styles.

Gender in educational leadership

Not only do most leadership theories deny the experience of women in school, theories of leadership are fraught with biases and unspoken assumptions about the role of gender in organizations. Most theory has focused only on males in organizations (Schmuck, 1996, p. 346).

Women in the UK and elsewhere may numerically dominate the teaching profession, but they are relatively rare in positions of authority, particularly in secondary schools, colleges, universities and in local administration of education, although this is not entirely true for schools in Israel (Goldring and Chen, 1994).

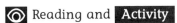 Reading and **Activity**

**Before continuing, we suggest you read the chapter by Marianne Coleman, 'Women in educational management', Chapter 9 in Bush, T. and West-Burnham, J. (eds.) *The Principles of Educational Management.*

This chapter starts by considering the themes of equity and career progress for women, but we suggest you pay particular attention to the section that introduces the concept of 'feminine' and 'masculine' styles of management and points out the link between 'feminine' management and effective schools.

❑ Comment

Those aspects of leadership and management regarded as 'feminine' are similar to those that are now identified as effective. In addition, the limited empirical evidence available (p. 191) appears to suggest that most women in leadership do operate in a style that is likely to empower others and to be strong in terms of communication with both staff and students. Such a style is likely to be both transformational and educative.

There are gender stereotypes associated with leadership. The numbers of men in senior management provide an image which may be self-perpetuating: 'Many more models of men headteachers are available to selectors, as a basis for stereotypes.' (Morgan *et al.*, 1983, p. 77). The stereotype is underpinned by: 'the unwarranted assumption that leadership is a male characteristic demanding physical and mental toughness and the ability to approach difficulties unemotionally' (Gane and Morgan, 1992, p. 53).

The existence of the stereotype that identifies leaders as males is supported by research in management undertaken in the 1970s and repeated in the 1990s: 'One of the most important hurdles for women in management in all countries has been thought to be the persistent stereotype that associates management with being male' (Schein, 1994, p. 47). The finding of Schein's research (*ibid.*, p. 48) was that both men and women tended to see the key characteristics of good managers as being:

Leadership Ability,

Desires Responsibility,

Skilled in Business Matters and

Analytical Ability.

Women were seen by both men and other women as less likely to have these characteristics. There is a stereotype of a tough, possibly aggressive, leader who is preoccupied with tasks rather than relationships. In contrast, the female manager in education has tended to be identified with the 'softer' aspects of management, for example, those aspects related to pastoral work or the management of people.

Research in the Shaanxi Province of China showed that:

> Management and leadership appear to be firmly identified with the male role in society, and the achievement of a management role as an indicator of male success. Female participation in management may then be seen as a type of 'role displacement', and, where it exists, lead to social pressure on both male and female. In addition there is the commonly held belief that women are less likely to see the wider picture, and are better at detail, implying the greater appropriateness of a subservient role (Coleman *et al.*, 1998, p. 154).

In the study of men and women in education in African countries, Sri Lanka, Malaysia and Hong Kong, Davies and Gunawardena (adapted from 1992, pp. 82, 85) identified areas of difference between the males and females. These included:

1. that men were more concerned with finance and salaries than women, who were more concerned with people within the school and their own workload;
2. 'the striking competitiveness of the male.' In contrast the women were more concerned with co-operation and sharing, and in teamwork;
3. men tend to be completely satisfied with their work, women more hesitant;
4. men wanted status and recognition, whilst women 'do not seem to want to be a subject of status envy'.

However, the conclusion (*ibid.*, p. 88) is not that all men and all women are in opposed camps, but that some men tend to have dominated the culture of power and of education: 'Hence the hierarchical, status-oriented, vertically differentiated institution comes to be taken as the "natural" way of organising large numbers of people; and that everything revolves around winning and losing is equally seen as "natural" to humanity rather than representing only one particular form of masculinity.'

Schmuck (1996, p. 355) claims that women act as both 'insiders' and 'outsiders' in educational organisations:

as insiders they [women] adopt the roles, norms, behaviours and expectations of the role they occupy as principals or superintendents. But, because the conditions of social gender roles demand it, they remain 'outsiders' because they do not reflect the cultural expectations of the role of leader as male. Women administrators are marginal. Women who are administrators must find new ways to behave because they do not meet the cultural expectations of being male in the leadership role.

❏ Female leadership

Empirical work with female principals and other female senior managers does indicate that they tend towards a participative and transformative management style. The majority (about 85%) of the female secondary headteachers of England and Wales (Coleman, 2000) perceived themselves as having a collaborative and people-centred style of management. This perception was stronger amongst the younger age group – those under, rather than over, 50 years of age. The people-centred style of management was endorsed by a study of female managers in business environments in Hong Kong and China (Chow and Luk, 1996, p. 35). This study indicated that the women gave top rating to motivators that related to personal relationships such as 'recognition for good work', and 'having a good relationship with superiors and colleagues.'

The identification of a collaborative style of management with the way women manage is in accord with a range of earlier findings. Research on female headteachers and principals in the USA, the UK, Australia, New Zealand and Canada appears to indicate that female managers are likely to work in a co-operative style, empowering their colleagues and making use of teamwork (Blackmore, 1989; Hall, 1996; Jirasinghe and Lyons, 1996). In a large-scale study of male and female primary and secondary heads in England, Jirasinghe and Lyons (1996) administered a variety of well tried personality tests, including the Occupational Personality Questionnaire (OPQ), the Belbin Team Types Questionnaire, and a leadership styles questionnaire derived from the work of Bass (1981). In terms of the OPQ dimensions female heads (both primary and secondary) described themselves as more:

- affiliative
- democratic
- caring
- artistic
- behavioural
- detail conscious
- conscientious, and worrying.

They tend to prefer the (Belbin) team role of:

- team worker,
- completer.

They identified themselves as participative and consultative leaders.

Male heads perceived themselves as more:

- data rational
- relaxed
- tough minded
- active
- competitive.

They did not show a particular preference in team roles; they identified themselves as delegative leaders.

Whilst participative and consultative and delegative leaders may be considered as similar in terms of not being autocratic, there are considerable differences in the way female and male heads perceived themselves: 'Female heads claim a preference for a style of leadership which favours consensus decision making; seeking the involvement of all relevant colleagues thereby securing their commitment and motivation; and a warm and friendly social style' (Jirasinghe and Lyons, 1996, p. 61).

The male heads choice of delegatory leadership did not imply the same level of empowerment and involvement of staff:

> Delegative leaders believe in delegation of tasks and responsibility. They tend to communicate less with their staff and are inclined not to give clearly defined instructions or plan the work of the personnel they oversee. Such leaders tend not to seek the staffs' views as to how projects should be conducted, but are inclined simply to hand over the work to be done (*ibid.*).

Shakeshaft (1989) reviews the research undertaken in the USA, which identifies the following with regard to the differences between women and men in management:

- Women tend to have more contact with both superordinates and subordinates, teachers and students.
- Women spend more time with community members and with colleagues, although these are usually other women.
- They are more informal.
- They are concerned with the individual differences between students.
- They view their position as that of an educational leader rather than a manager, and see the job as a service to the community.
- There may be less acceptance of female than of male leaders amongst both men and women; female leaders may therefore live in a world that 'carries an undercurrent of stress and anxiety' (*ibid.* pp. 175).
- They may gain more satisfaction from supervising instruction, and men more from administration.
- In communication they may appear to be more polite and tentative than men, using qualifiers to simple statements. Body language may also be different, indicating a lower status for women.
- Women tend to use more participatory styles of management, and use collaborative strategies to resolve conflict.

❏ Feminine and masculine

Rather than referring to men and women or male and female, the term 'gender' (when applied to social roles) can be relatively value free. In this sense 'masculine' need not apply exclusively to men nor 'feminine' to women: '"Masculine" and "feminine" represent coherent, consistent "ideal types", which none of us are. Gender is not defined by physical sex so an individual may have a very clear identity as a man (male) while having a largely "feminine" behaviour repertoire' (Gray, 1989, p. 43).

Gray (1993) has identified two paradigms which can be used as a means of examining gender issues, including management, in schools (see Coleman, 1994b, p. 189). The types of qualities listed by Gray need not be mutually exclusive; each person can recognise he or she has qualities from both lists. The Bem Sex Role Inventory developed for use in psychology (Bem, 1974) also identifies groups of attributes associated with masculine and feminine behaviour. Research undertaken by Bem (1974) and endorsed by Ferrario (1994), indicated that the most effective leaders were those who had many qualities from both lists, and it termed these effective leaders 'androgynous' leaders.

The male and female paradigms developed by Gray were used in interviews with five female headteachers of mixed secondary schools in one county (Coleman, 1996) and in a survey of all female secondary headteachers of England and Wales (Coleman, 2000). In both cases the results show a predominance of 'feminine' qualities amongst the female headteachers, but the choice is heavily tempered by the inclusion of some 'masculine' qualities. The qualities listed in Table 4.1 present an empirically based alternative to the feminine paradigm identified by Gray (1993).

Table 4.1   Qualities identified by 50% or more of the headteachers

Quality		%
Aware of individual differences	(f)	86.0
Caring	(f)	79.4
Intuitive	(f)	76.2
Tolerant	(f)	68.7
Creative	(f)	63.0
Evaluative	(m)	61.1
Disciplined	(m)	60.4
Informal	(f)	59.4
Competitive	(m)	50.6
Objective	(m)	50.6

Total = 470; (f) = feminine, (m) = masculine.
Source: Gray (1993).

Overall, it would appear that there is a strong identification with most of the feminine traits on the part of the headteachers, and a weak identification with most of the masculine traits. However, there are a number of masculine traits, specifically 'evaluative', 'disciplined', 'competitive' and 'objective', which are identified by 50% or more of the respondents. In addition there are two feminine traits that were identified by very few of the respondents: 'subjective' and 'non-competitive'. These deviations from the stereotypes temper the picture of a pure feminine paradigm of management style amongst the female secondary headteachers of England and Wales and indicate a more androgynous style of management.

❏ The contribution of women to leadership

Alongside the recognition of the lack of opportunities for women, there is also recognition of qualities women may bring to management and leadership. Reflecting on women in educational management, Ozga (1993, p. 15) concludes: 'We do not suggest that women have a "natural" capacity to manage better, but we do submit that the styles of communication and organization with which women are familiar are effective management styles, with particular application in education.'

Shakeshaft (1989, p. 186) concludes from her review of the empirical studies that: 'women's traditional and stereotypic styles of communication are more like those of a good manager than are men's stereotypic styles.'

It would appear to be the case that there is an identifiable style of management that can be deemed 'feminine' and that this style of management is more likely to be found amongst women. Current thinking on leadership would tend to identify many aspects of the feminine style with effectiveness in education. Many women leaders appear to adopt a style that could be termed transformational and educative.

Stereotypes and theories about leadership are still predominantly male. However, there is a growing body of research evidence that shows that the experience and attitudes of women are different from men, and that a single male model of educational leadership is inadequate. In addition, the research evidence indicates that women are able to bring strengths to leadership and management which may be particularly appropriate to effective educational leadership today.

Activity

Return to the list of generalisations about leadership given earlier in this chapter derived from the current literature (p. 22). When you reread the list in the context of this book as a whole, it is clear there is a view of what constitutes a good leader in education today. Leadership is not confined to the principal or headteacher, but may be most strongly identified at this level or amongst other senior managers. As we have seen, in transformational cultures, leadership is likely to be devolved.

Considering the context of your school or college, try to identify examples or illustrations for the list of generalisations.

❑ Comment

It is unlikely you have found examples for all the generalisations from within your own institution. Beare *et al.* (1993, p. 147) do provide illustrations for the generalisations; in the case of three generalisations:

2. Outstanding leaders have a vision for their organisation (principal envisages school as a learning centre for whole community).
6. The leader has an important role in developing culture of organisation (principal involves members of community in all ceremonies at the school).
10. Both 'masculine' and 'feminine' stereotype qualities are important in leadership, regardless of the gender of the leader (principal is sensitive and caring about personal needs ('feminine' stereotype); principal fosters competitive, team approach in raising school's academic standing ('masculine stereotype')).

Leadership and roles

In the discussion of leadership, we have occasionally referred to the 'role' of the leader without specifically defining the term 'role'. There is an important distinction to be made between leadership or management position and the roles of people occupying such positions. Burnham (1969, pp. 72–3) clarifies the distinction:

> The positions are collections of rights and duties, distinguished from one another, and designated by a title such as principal, deputy head or teacher … Within the organisation, positions are ordered hierarchically in terms of status, and may be thought of as locations on an organisational chart.

> Associated with every position in an organisation is a set of expectations concerning what is appropriate behaviour for a person occupying that position, and those appropriate behaviours comprise the role associated with the office. In order to differentiate these two terms – position and role – one might say that a person occupies a position but plays or performs a role … a role is the dynamic aspect of position.

A job specification set out by the head or principal or other senior staff therefore does not, by itself, constitute the role definition. The job specification is only the starting point for the negotiation of role, which is a continuing process involving all members of the role incumbent's role set.

A role set comprises those people who have the ability to influence the ways in which roles are performed. The role set is likely to include the post-holder's immediate superordinate and direct subordinates. It may also include others holding the same or similar positions and others with a legitimate right to influence a particular role.

Coulson (1974, pp. 6–7) applies the concept of role set to the position of deputy head in an English primary school:

The deputy head in a primary school will perceive that certain people will have legitimate rights to hold expectations for his position. These persons will constitute his 'role set'. The deputy head's role set includes the teachers in the school, the caretaker, the pupils, the parents, deputy heads of other schools and so on. Cain (1968) suggests two criteria for 'effective role definers': (a) those likely to be affected in some way by the role behaviour engaged in; and (b) those from this group with some power over the actor in the relevant area of action...The influence of the role set is complicated by the possibility that what really matters is not the actual expectations of the members of the role set but the deputy head's perception of their expectations.

The concept of role set appears to accord little value to the role incumbent's own assessment of how his or her role should be performed. In practice, however, the post-holder usually has clear views about the nature of the role, based on several years of professional experience. This personal conception links with the perceived views of the role set to determine how the role will be played in each individual case. Hall (1997, p. 63) refers to the concepts of 'role-taking and role-making': 'the reasons why an individual behaves differently from his or her formal job description may derive from the individual's attempts to make the role his or her own, by fitting it to his or her own interpretation.'

The influence of the individual is at its most evident when a new person takes up a position. The differences between former and present incumbents can be ascribed to different personal assessments of how the role should be played and to differences in perceptions about the collective views of the role set.

Where there are differences between the views of the role holder and members of the role set, or where there are tensions within the role, the role holder can experience role conflict or role strain. The role of the lecturer and of the middle manager in both further and higher education has been subject to change and redefinition. In a study of the role of the head of department at the 'new' universities in England, Smith (1996, p. 248) identified 'the rapid rate of change and difficult economic climate in higher education' as one of the main causes of pressure. He sees the main sources of role conflict as:

> the difficult balance of representing the department and its staff to the university and, at the same time, the university to the department; the difficulty of managing academics, particularly in the areas of staff discipline and resolving conflicts between staff; acquiring and managing resources in a very difficult economic climate (*ibid.*).

The demands of the post are considerable and varied. In one of the case studies undertaken by Smith (*ibid.* p. 200), a dean listed her expectations of the head of department:

> I have so many. They're highly paid. I expect them to manage and lead their departments effectively; manage, lead and develop their staff effectively; be responsive to change; be proactive and not reactive to things that happen to us; to be corporate, to run a department within a university; to understand and implement the mission, to use the mission as a starting point.

> I expect heads to be able to delegate and not to think that it's more important to deal with that urgent letter rather than, say, have a view of the Faculty strategic research plan up to the year 2000.

A study of the role perceptions of government and non-government headteachers in Pakistan (Simkins *et al.*, 1998) found that the headteachers' perception of their role was influenced by external constraints and pressures. In particular the differences between the government and non-government schools: 'affect the demands and constraints under which headteachers work, both objectively – for example, in permitting or proscribing freedom in particular areas – and subjectively in creating expectations among headteachers about how they should play their roles' (*ibid.*, p. 144).

Grace (1995) reports on the tensions experienced by headteachers as a result of the change in culture away from the co-operation experienced previously to a time of increased competitiveness between schools. Hall (1997) comments on the possibility of role strain for both headteachers and governors as a result of the changes in the power and responsibilities of school governors in England and Wales. However, it is also possible that headteachers may welcome changes of this kind in view of the additional freedom they may experience in being able to redefine their own roles to some extent.

One potential area of role strain for headteachers has been identified by Hughes (1989, p. 11) as the dual role model, where:

> the chief executive of a professionally staffed organisation may also be considered to be its leading professional. An essential element in the model is the close interdependency of the two aspects. This is demonstrated in relation to school headship, but is equally applicable at other levels and in different types of educational organisation.

Although it may be useful to consider these two aspects of an educational leader independently, research with headteachers showed that there was:

> considerable inter-penetration of the two sub-roles. It seems that the professional-as-administrator does not act in some matters as a leading professional and in others as a chief executive. Professional knowledge skills and attitudes are likely to have a profound effect on the whole range of tasks undertaken by the head of a professional organisation (*ibid.*, p. 15).

A move towards greater autonomy of schools in South Africa was evidenced by the creation of Model C schools where the school took more responsibility for finance. The redefinition of role from leading professional to chief executive that was implied by the change was clear:

> All the principals agreed that new functions have been assigned to them since the implementation of Model C. According to them they now had to fulfil the role of manager of the school. It was felt that their role had changed from an 'instructional leader' to a 'manager', and said that this included the role of 'director' and 'financial expert'. One interviewee regretted that he did not have time to visit teachers or walk around on school premises any more, since his administrative tasks increasingly confined him to the office. Another principal felt that he had now become a 'general manager': a personnel, financial, site and instructional manager (Steyn and Squelch, 1994, p. 186).

The National Standards for Headteachers (TTA, 1998) refers to the headteacher as 'the leading professional in the school' and in the UK the role of the principal or headteacher is now more clearly defined than previously. The development of headteacher training and competencies (*ibid.*), and the demands of external inspection and other statutory controls, have focused attention on the role of the head:

> Earlier research showed the head's role to be poorly defined, with inadequate preparation, and performed in an ad hoc rather than a strategic manner (e.g. Hall et al, 1986). In the 1990s, headteachers are more likely to have job descriptions and expanded opportunities for training and development...Unlike other management roles (e.g. deputy headteachers and middle managers), the head's role has been subject to intense scrutiny (Hall, 1997, p. 66).

Activity

Consider the role played by a senior manager with leadership responsibilities in your school or college. Try to identify the members of the role set and the range of internal and external influences and expectations that may influence the role. Alternatively, interview the senior manager and ask for his or her views.

❑ Comment

The members of the role set will obviously include all those who work closely with the individual leader. They are also likely to include some of the following: students; parents; support staff; representatives of external agencies; employers and other members of the community; their own family; and the previous incumbent of the job.

Hall (1997, p. 62) outlines some of the external influences that cause difficulties in attempting to identify the nature of management and leadership roles:

These difficulties arise from a number of sources, including the diversity of goals in education, teachers' perceptions of themselves as 'professionals' and the interaction of central government's prescriptions and individual teachers' interpretations. Additionally, there are the global changes that influence teachers' work and culture in the post-modern age.

❏ Building on key learning points

- Whilst leadership theory tends to be based on western models, a range of practice is likely to be found in different cultures.
- Leadership and management are different concepts but are generally found within the same role.
- Studies of leadership in education endorse transformational leadership, educative leadership and an awareness of the moral dimension of leadership.
- An increase in autonomy for educational institutions poses additional challenges for leaders, including the need to take responsibility for strategic leadership.
- Feminine qualities of leadership and management differ from the stereotypes of leadership, but have similarity to those styles of leadership and management generally considered effective.
- The role of the leader is a larger concept than that of job definition.
- Role stress may be caused by conflict of views and by the impact of changes in the external environment.

5. Organisational theory and strategic management

This chapter considers:

- theory in educational management;
- models of educational management;
- organisational culture; and
- using theory to improve practice.

Introduction

In this chapter, we assess the significance of organisational theory for the development of strategy and effective practice in educational institutions. We examine six broad models of educational management and link them to aims, structure and the external environment. We consider whether it is possible to integrate these models and conclude by discussing how an appreciation of theory may be used to improve management practice.

The theory/practice divide

Management is often regarded as a practical activity. The determination of aims, the allocation of resources and the evaluation of effectiveness all involve action. Practitioners tend to be dismissive of theories and concepts for their alleged remoteness from the 'real' school situation. Hughes (1985, pp. 3, 31) accepts that links between theory and practice have been weak: 'Theory and practice are uneasy, uncomfortable bedfellows, particularly when one is attempting to understand the complexities of human behaviour in organizational settings...It has been customary for practitioners to state the dichotomy in robust terms: airy-fairy theory versus down-to-earth practice.'

The mutual suspicion suggested by these comments leads to a theory/practice 'divide'. Theory may be perceived as esoteric and remote from practice. Yet the acid test of theory should be its applicability to practice. Theory is valuable and relevant if it serves to explain practice and provide managers with a guide to action:

> Theories are most useful for influencing practice when they suggest new ways in which events and situations can be perceived. Fresh insight may be provided by focusing attention on possible interrelationships that the practitioner has failed to notice, and which can be further explored and tested through empirical research. If the result is a better understanding of practice, the theory–practice gap is significantly reduced for those concerned. Theory cannot then be dismissed as irrelevant (Hughes and Bush, 1991, p. 234).

The relevance of theory to good practice

When a teacher or a manager takes a decision, it reflects in part that person's view of the organisation. Such views or preconceptions are coloured by experience and by the attitudes engendered by that experience. These attitudes take on the character of frames of reference, or theories, which necessarily influence the decision-making process. Personal theories may be regarded as a product of experience.

Theory serves to provide a basis for decision-making. Managerial activity is enhanced by an explicit awareness of the theoretical framework underpinning practice in educational institutions. As a result, some academics and practitioners 'vigorously challenge the traditional view that practical on the job experience on its own provides adequate management training in education' (Hughes, 1984, p. 5).

There are four main arguments to support the view that managers have much to learn from an appreciation of theory:

- A frame of reference is required to provide the insight for decision-making. This frame provides the basis for interpreting events and problems as they occur. Frames, or theories, are underpinned by values which, in turn, inform the generation of strategy.
- Dependence on personal experience in interpreting events is narrow because it discards the knowledge of others. Familiarity with the arguments and insights of theorists enables the practitioner to deploy a wide range of experience and understanding in resolving the problems of today.
- Errors of judgement can occur while experience is being acquired. Mistakes are costly in both human and material terms. Resources are limited but the needs of children and students are even more important. Appreciation of theory, which might be regarded as the distilled experience of others, helps to overcome the potential risks of limited experience.
- Experience may be particularly unhelpful as the sole guide to action when the practitioner begins to operate in a different context. Organisational variables may mean that practice in one school or college has little relevance in the new environment. A broader awareness of theory and practice may be valuable as the manager attempts to interpret behaviour in the fresh situation (Bush 1995, pp. 18–19).

The nature of theory in educational management

There is no single theory of educational management. This is because it comprises a series of perspectives rather than an all-embracing 'scientific' truth:

[Theories] 'describe' or operate in a social or political world that is itself changing...The perspectives rest more upon a professional consensus of what is possible and relevant and valued than upon a scientific consensus as to what is true...The perspective is a 'way of seeing' a problem rather than a rigid set of rules and procedures (House, 1981, p. 20).

The existence of several different perspectives creates what Bolman and Deal (1984) describe as 'conceptual pluralism'. Each theory has something to offer in explaining behaviour and events in educational institutions.

Morgan (1986) also emphasises the diversity of theories of management and organisation. He uses 'metaphors' to explain 'the complex and paradoxical character of organizational life' (*ibid.*, p. 13):

Theories and explanations of organizational life are based on metaphors that lead us to see and understand organizations in distinctive yet partial ways...the use of metaphor implies a way of thinking and a way of seeing that pervades how we understand our world...metaphor...always produces this kind of one-sided insight. In highlighting certain interpretations it tends to force others into a background role (*ibid.*, 1986, pp. 12–13).

This phenomenon may mean that participants in a meeting, for example, may interpret the same events in different ways. This is because people tend to focus on those aspects that fit their conceptual framework and ignore other aspects. Arguably, the most effective managers are those who are able to perceive events from a number of different perspectives and 'shift frames' as appropriate during the course of events. We shall illustrate this issue later in this chapter.

Educational management theories tend to be normative in that they reflect beliefs about the nature of educational institutions and the behaviour of individuals within them. When, for example, practitioners or academics claim that decisions in schools are reached following a participative process, they may be expressing normative judgements rather than analysing actual practice. Theories are also selective or partial in that they emphasise certain aspects of the institution at the expense of other elements. The support of one theoretical model leads to the neglect of other approaches. Schools and colleges are arguably too complex to be capable of analysis through a single dimension.

Models of educational management

Many different theories have been discussed by various writers on educational management. These can be classified into several broad models (Bush, 1995). Five of these models are discussed in the next reading.

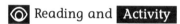 Reading and Activity

Please now read pp. 36–47 of Tony Bush's 'Theory and practice in educational management', Chapter 2 in Bush, T. and West-Burnham, J. (eds.) *Principles of Educational Management*.

This section summarises the main features of five models of management. As you read, compare the models in respect of their treatment of three important aspects of schools or colleges, all of which are significant for strategic management:

- goals or aims
- organisational structure
- the external environment.

Our comments are shown below but please do not read them until you have completed the activity. The reading features five models of educational management but does not deal with the increasingly important cultural model which will be examined later in this chapter.

❏ Comment

These two important aspects of school and college management illustrate the many differences among the five models. There is increasing emphasis on goals in the literature on school improvement: 'School leaders must [identify] short-term, manageable goals which are in line with the overall direction of the school' (Blum and Butler, 1989, p. 19).

Bureaucratic models claim that organisations pursue goals set by their leaders. Collegial models emphasise shared objectives, while political theories assume that goals may be contested by interest groups. Subjective models stress the primacy of individual aims and deny the validity of the concept of organisational goals. Ambiguity theories claim that goals are problematic and unclear.

The treatment of organisational structure also varies significantly among the five models. There is a tension between the emphasis on structure and the alternative focus on the behaviour of people who 'occupy' organisational roles. Bureaucratic models stress the importance of structure and emphasise hierarchical authority and 'top-down' decisions. Collegial theories prefer to focus on lateral relationships between professionals who all possess authority of expertise. In political models, the structure may become the battleground for competing factions. Subjective models stress the personal qualities of individuals rather than their position within the formal structure. Ambiguity theories emphasise the fluid nature of participation in committees and the unpredictability of outcomes.

Relationships with the external environment are increasingly significant for a strategic approach to management, as Wong *et al.* (1998) suggest (see p. 15), but these links are portrayed in very different ways by the various models, as Bush (1995, p. 145) explains:

> Some of the formal approaches tend to regard schools and colleges as 'closed systems', relatively impervious to outside influences. Other formal theories typify educational organizations as 'open systems', responding to the needs of their communities and building a positive image to attract new clients.
>
> Collegial models tend to be inadequate in explaining relationships with the environment. Policy is thought to be determined within a participatory framework which can make it difficult to locate responsibility for decisions. Heads may be held accountable for outcomes which do not enjoy their personal support, a position which is difficult to sustain for both the leader and the external group. Collegial approaches gloss over this difficulty by the unrealistic assumption that heads are always in agreement with decisions.
>
> Political models tend to portray relationships with the environment as unstable. External bodies are regarded as interest groups which may participate in the complex bargaining process that characterizes decision-making. Internal and external groups may form alliances to press for the adoption of certain policies. Interaction with the environment is seen as a central aspect of an essentially political decision process.
>
> In subjective models, the environment is treated as a prime source of the meanings placed on events by people within the organization. Individuals are thought to interpret situations in different ways and these variations in meaning are attributed in part to the different external influences upon participants.
>
> Ambiguity models regard the environment as a source of the uncertainty which contributes to the unpredictability of organizations. The signals from outside groups are often unclear and contradictory, leading to confusion inside schools and colleges. Interpretation of messages from a turbulent environment may be difficult, adding to the ambiguity of the decision process.

The differences among the five models in these three respects are summarised in Table 5.1.

Table 5.1   Differences among the five models of management

Elements of management	Type of model				
	Formal	Collegial	Political	Subjective	Ambiguity
Levels at which goals are determined	Institutional	Institutional	Subunit	Individual	Unclear
Process by which goals are determined	Set by leaders	Agreement	Conflict	Problematic; may be imposed by leaders	Unpredictable
Nature of structure	Objective reality; hierarchical	Objective reality; lateral	Setting for subunit conflict	Constructed through human interaction	Problematic
Links with environment	May be 'closed' or open; head accountable	Accountability blurred by shared decision-making	Unstable; external bodies portrayed as interest groups	Source of individual meanings	Source of uncertainty

Source: Adapted from Bush (1995, p. 147).

Organisational culture

Organisational culture is the sixth theoretical model but is given separate consideration here because of its increasing importance in the literature. Culture relates to the informal aspects of organisations rather than their official elements which are often typified by portrayals of structure. Culture focuses on the values, beliefs and norms of individuals and how these perceptions coalesce into shared organisational meanings. O'Neill (1994, p. 103) explains the contemporary significance of this concept:

> The importance of understanding organisational culture lies in the notion that the officially agreed and sanctioned areas of organisational activity produce only a partial picture of how and why an organisation functions as it does. Educational managers, therefore, need an analytical framework in order to identify the undocumented, unofficial and intangible elements which influence the way the organisation functions.

The following definitions capture the essence of this important concept:

> Organisational culture is the characteristic spirit and belief of an organisation, demonstrated, for example, in the norms and values that are generally held about how people should treat each other, the nature of working relationships that should be developed and attitudes to change. These norms are deep, taken-for-granted assumptions that are not always expressed, and are often known without being understood (Torrington and Weightman, 1989, p. 18).

> An increasing number of writers...have adopted the term 'culture' to define that social and phenomenological uniqueness of a particular organisational community...we have finally acknowledged publicly that uniqueness is a virtue, that values are important and that they should be fostered (Beare *et al.*, 1989a, p. 173).

> Cultural models assume that beliefs, values and ideology are at the heart of organisations. Individuals hold certain ideas and value-preferences which influence how they behave and how they view the behaviour of other members. These norms become shared traditions which are communicated within the group and are reinforced by symbols and ritual (Bush, 1995, p. 130).

O'Neill (1994, p. 105) refers to Deal's (1988) discussion of several elements of culture which are enacted in a variety of ways:

- shared values and beliefs expressed in written form
- heroes and heroines who typify desirable organisational behaviours and personal qualities
{
- rituals which allow members to come together and reinforce core values
- ceremonies which celebrate those values
}
- stories which communicate and disseminate philosophy and successful practice
- an informal network of cultural players which serves to maintain the culture in the face of pressures for change

The reference to 'shared values and beliefs' serves to emphasise the normative nature of organisational culture. We noted earlier that educational management theories tend to be normative and this may be particularly true of culture. In practice, particularly in large schools and colleges, there may be several subcultures based on the professional and personal interests of different groups. Departments,for example, are likely to have sectional interests which may be expressed in demands for additional resources. These subunits often have internal coherence but weak links to other groups in the organisation. Wallace and Hall's (1994, pp. 28, 127) research on school management teams (SMTs) in England and Wales suggests they have clear internal norms but that this may be at the expense of good relationships with other colleagues:

> SMTs...developed a 'culture of teamwork': shared beliefs and values about working together to manage the school. Beliefs and values include those relating to norms, or rules of behaviour. A norm common to the SMTs...was that decisions must be reached by achieving a working consensus, entailing the acknowledgement of any dissenting views. Where the meanings and norms held by one individual are shared with others, they belong to a common culture...There was a clear distinction between interaction inside the team and contact with those outside...to the extent that they were excluded from the inner world of the team.

⊙ Reading

Please now read pp. 32–6 of Tony Bush's 'Organisational culture and strategic management', Chapter 3 in Middlewood, D. and Lumby, J. (eds.) *Strategic Management in Schools and Colleges*. This provides a useful overview of the meaning and main features of organisational culture in education.

Organisational culture and strategic management

It has become received wisdom that an ability both to appreciate and interpret culture is a valuable, if not essential, component of effective management. Because it is deeply embedded in organisations, understanding culture is a long-term process. The subtlety of individual and shared values and beliefs means they are deeply ingrained in many schools and colleges. This does not necessarily mean that culture is impervious to change but modifying it is likely to be a difficult challenge for leaders. Culture and strategy have certain features in common, not least because both are usually organisation-wide phenomena, and their development takes time.

⊙ Reading and Activity

Please now read pp. 38–44 of Tony Bush's 'Organisational culture and strategic management', Chapter 3 in Middlewood, D. and Lumby, J. (eds.) *Strategic Management in Schools and Colleges*.

As you read, consider the relationship between culture and strategy and assess how culture may contribute to strategic management.

Our comments are shown below but please do not read them until you have completed the activity.

❏ Comments
Bush suggests four ways in which culture and strategy are linked:

- Both are underpinned by values and beliefs.
- Culture is an important dimension of the context within which strategy operates.
- Both operate or develop over extended timescales.
- Both tend to relate to the whole organisation but tolerance, or celebration, of sub-cultures may be a valuable feature of strategic management, particularly in larger schools and colleges.

Bush also puts forward four ways in which leaders may take account of culture in developing their strategies for school or college development:

- Auditing or diagnosing culture.
- Generating new or modified culture through espousing and communicating a vision based on clearly articulated values.
- Taking account of the prevailing culture in developing strategy but also seeking to modify culture if it is inconsistent with new strategic aims.
- Using their power as leaders to change or 'found' culture.

Conceptual pluralism

The six perspectives discussed in this chapter represent different ways of looking at educational institutions. In certain circumstances one model may appear to be applicable while another perspective may seem more appropriate in a different setting. There is no single approach capable of presenting a complete framework for our understanding of educational institutions: 'The search for an all-encompassing model is simplistic, for no one model can delineate the intricacies of decision processes in complex organisations' (Baldridge *et al.*, 1978 p. 28).

Bureaucratic and other formal models dominated the early stages of theory development in educational management. Formal structure, rational decision-making and 'top-down' leadership were regarded as the central concepts of effective management and attention was given to refining these processes to increase efficiency. Since the 1970s, however, there has been a gradual realisation that formal models are 'at best partial and at worst grossly deficient' (Chapman, 1993, p. 215).

The other models featured in this volume all developed in response to the perceived weaknesses of what was then regarded as conventional theory. They have demonstrated the limitations of the formal models but they are no less partial than the theory their advocates seek to replace. There is more theory and, by exploring different dimensions of management, its total explanatory power is greater than that provided by any single model: 'Traditional views . . . still dominate understandings of theory, research and administrative practice [but] there are now systematic alternatives to this approach. As a result, educational administration is now theoretically much richer, more diverse and complex than at any other time in its short history' (Evers and Lakomski, 1991, p. 99).

All the perspectives are limited in that they do not give a complete picture of educational institutions. Rather they turn the spotlight on particular aspects of the organisation and consequently leave other features in the shade.

The increased emphasis on strategic planning in the 1990s has led to a renewed interest in formal models and particularly rational decision-making processes. Levačić (1995, p. 61) shows that, in England and Wales, local management of schools was underpinned from the outset by 'the promotion of rational processes and techniques'. What Levačić (*ibid.*) describes as 'the official blueprint for local management' was set out in an official report by Coopers & Lybrand (1988) and is essentially rational. Levačić (1995, p. 62) questions 'whether the rational model of decision-making is far too idealised to be of any use in practice', echoing the reservations discussed in this chapter, but there is little doubt that strategic management is based on rational assumptions.

We have already discussed the relationship between strategy and organisational culture but leaders need to be aware of other models in managing strategic change. To be locked into the rational model is like playing golf with one club; you might complete the round but you will not optimise your score. Conceptual pluralism enables managers to select and use the most appropriate model for the problem or situation they face. Examples for each of the models include the following:

- The collegial model is appropriate where staff 'ownership' of change is critical to its successful implementation.
- The political model is relevant where negotiation with subunits is likely to be a valuable element of decision-making.
- The subjective model helps managers to appreciate that teachers and other staff may have a unique perspective on the organisation and events within it.
- The ambiguity model is helpful in managing environmental turbulence.
- The cultural model is valuable in helping managers to acknowledge the beliefs and values of staff and stakeholders.

Using theory to improve practice

The six models present different approaches to the management of education but the ultimate test of theory is whether it improves practice. Theory which is remote from practice will not improve school or college management, or the central activity of teaching and learning.

There should be little doubt about the potential for theory to inform practice. School and college managers generally engage in a process of implicit theorising in deciding how to formulate policy or respond to events:

> There is a close relationship between the way we think and the way we act...Our images or metaphors are theories or conceptual frameworks. Practice is never theory-free, for it is always guided by an image of what one is trying to do. The real issue is whether or not we are aware of the theory guiding our action (Morgan, 1986, pp. 335–6).

Theory provides the analytical basis for determining a response to events and helps in the interpretation of management information. Facts cannot simply be left to speak for themselves. They require the explanatory framework of theory in order to ascertain their real meaning.

The multiplicity of competing models means that no single theory is sufficient to guide practice. Appreciation of various approaches, or 'conceptual pluralism' (Bolman and Deal, 1984), is the starting point for effective action. It provides a 'conceptual tool-kit' for the manager to deploy as appropriate in addressing problems and developing strategy. Bush (1995, p. 154) illustrates this eclectic approach by reference to the chair's role in meetings:

> The chair may begin by adopting the normatively preferable collegial model, particularly if there is a culture of collaboration in the school or college. If consensus cannot be achieved, the chair may need to adopt the political strategy of mediation to achieve a compromise. If the emerging outcome appears to contradict governing body policy, it may be necessary to stress accountability, a central concept in the formal model. Throughout the discussion, there may be different interpretations of the same phenomena and sensitivity may be required to this essentially subjective position. There may also be elements of the ambiguity model, particularly if there is fluid participation in the discussion.

Morgan (1986, p. 322) argues that organisational analysis based on these multiple perspectives comprises two elements:

- A diagnostic reading of the situation being investigated, using different metaphors to identify or highlight key aspects of the situation,
- A critical evaluation of the significance of the different interpretations resulting from the diagnosis.

These skills are consistent with the concept of the 'reflective practitioner' whose managerial approach incorporates both good experience and a distillation of theory based on wide reading and discussion with both academics and fellow practitioners. This combination of theory and practice enables leaders to acquire the overview required for strategic management in the increasingly complex schools and colleges of the 1990s.

❑ Building on key learning points

- Organisational theory is valuable in helping to explain events and situations.
- There are several competing theories of educational management, leading to 'conceptual pluralism'.
- Organisational culture is increasingly important in acknowledging the unofficial and intangible aspects of schools and colleges.
- The dominant rational model has been adopted by policy-makers but it has certain limitations which make it inappropriate for certain situations, particularly in periods of rapid and multiple change.

6. The purpose of strategic management

This chapter considers:

- school and college effectiveness;
- school and college improvement;
- theories relating to quality including TQM; and
- re-engineering.

Introduction

Taking a strategic view about the future of an educational organisation involves consideration of aims and objectives for that organisation. The likelihood is that the aims of any school or college will specify, explicitly or implicitly, notions that relate to improvement, to increased effectiveness or to the search after quality. However, it is possible that these aims may be superficial and that progress towards the chosen ideal is minimal or non-existent. Harber and Davies (1997, p. 31), writing about school effectiveness in developing countries, point out that there may be vested interests on the part of individuals or government which prevent the whole-hearted adoption of ideals relating to improvement: 'One of the fatal flaws in school effectiveness and improvement programmes is the assumption that everyone – teachers, principals, governments – would like total school effectiveness but that they are merely prevented from achieving this through lack of resources or know-how. The reality is quite different.'

They point out that teachers may prefer to put some of their efforts into the earning of a second income through private tuition rather than into improving normal school provision and that governments may welcome research findings on the differential effectiveness of schools, since this may imply that faults lie with individual schools rather than the system, drawing 'attention away from the effects of poverty in the surrounding community, or from the effects of levels of state funding itself' (*ibid.*, p. 33).

Research into effectiveness may not be entirely relevant where problems are system wide, as is claimed in relation to the state schools in the United Arab Emirates: 'the entire state system of schooling is dominated by the problem of wastage, that is, progressive drop out, non-completion and repetition of years, to the point that only a relatively small proportion of each annual cohort of pupils who enter the system finally complete their studies' (Shaw *et al.*, 1995, p. 10).

Although there may be micro- or macro-political dimensions to the purposes of strategic management, in general, schools and colleges do aspire to improve or become more effective. In this chapter, consideration is given to the current understanding of effectiveness, improvement and quality management as they apply to educational institutions. Amongst the influences that have contributed to awareness of these concepts are the following:

- The growth in autonomy (identified in Chapter 2), which has meant that educational institutions are now taking responsibility for their own planning.
- An increase in the accountability of schools and colleges with an international move towards inspection (CERI, 1995), and a stress on performance exemplified by the 'league tables' in England and Wales and elsewhere, e.g. Singapore.

Alongside these international trends (Caldwell and Spinks, 1992) which have encouraged schools and colleges to take responsibility for planning, there has been an increased awareness of the impact of the individual institution on student achievement. Early research findings in the 1960s and 1970s had tended to show 'very limited school effects on academic outcomes and created a climate of professional educational opinion which held that variation in individual school organizations had minimal effects upon pupils' development' (Reynolds, 1992, p. 1).

Whilst the measurement of effectiveness is not without problems, it is now generally accepted that 'schools matter, that schools do have major effects upon children's development and that, to put it simply, schools do make a difference' (Reynolds and Creemers, 1990, p. 1).

This chapter will consider some of the ultimate purposes of strategic management, that is, the ways in which schools and colleges may plan and manage, to improve, or 'add-value' year on year to the education of young people and their preparation for future life. One of the most obvious areas that schools and colleges may target is their effectiveness, where an effective school is defined as: 'one in which pupils progress further than might be predicted from consideration of the attainment of its intake' (Sammons *et al.*, 1994, p. 2).

The concept of effectiveness

Effectiveness may be largely associated with classroom factors directly affecting teaching and learning. However, the co-ordination of such factors and the establishment of a culture which promotes them lie with the overall management and ethos of the school or college.

❏ The development of effectiveness research

A number of important research studies appeared in the late 1970s and early 1980s which emphasised the significance of the school as a variable in student achievement. Amongst the studies undertaken in the UK are those of Rutter *et al.* (1979), Mortimore *et al.* (1988) and Smith and Tomlinson (1989). Studies undertaken in a variety of contexts, on different age groups, and in different countries (the USA, The Netherlands, Canada, Australia and New Zealand), confirmed the existence of significant differences between schools in students achievements.

Research on school effectiveness has tended to concentrate on quantitative indicators, particularly examination results, and has also tended to look for clear links between identified factors and the greater achievement of students: 'school effectiveness refers to all theories and research studies concerning the means–ends relationships between educational processes and outcomes, in particular student knowledge and skills ... aiming at explanations for differences in student achievement between schools and classrooms' (Creemers and Reezigt, 1997, p. 401).

Although much of the literature on effectiveness is associated with schools, the achievement of colleges is also measured by quantitative means. For example, the work of the colleges of further education in England is measured by six performance indicators (FEFC, 1998):

- achievement of funding target;
- percentage change in student numbers;
- in-year retention rate;
- achievement rates;
- contribution to the national targets; and
- out-turn average level of funding.

The early concerns of school effectiveness researchers in the UK were often related to issues of equity. Sammons *et al.* (1995, p. 3) identify three important features of this early research which mainly focused on schools in disadvantaged areas:

- clientele (poor/ethnic minority children)
- subject matter (basic skills in reading and maths)
- equity (children of the urban poor should achieve at the same level as those of the middle class).

However, effectiveness research has now considered many areas, including the following:

- The stability of school effects over time.
- The consistency of school effects on different outcomes.
- The differential effects of schools on different groups of students, e.g. those of differing socioeconomic backgrounds.
- The differing size of school effects.
- Departmental differences in effectiveness (adapted from Reynolds *et al.*, 1996, pp. 136–7).

❏ Characteristics of effective schools

Whilst effectiveness may be considered at different levels or subunits within the institution, the reasons for greater progress in one school rather than another are at the heart of effectiveness. One of the main features of research in this area is the attempt to find causal factors leading to increased effectiveness. The outcomes of this research have tended to be presented in the form of factors common to effective schools. No two definitions of the characteristics of the effective school are exactly the same. None the less, a list which reflects international research and inspection evidence, and summarises mainly British research literature, provides a list of 11 key factors:

1.	Professional leadership	Firm and purposeful
		A participative approach
		The leading professional
2.	Shared vision and goals	Unity of purpose
		Consistency of practice
		Collegiality and collaboration
3.	A learning environment	An orderly atmosphere
		An attractive working environment
4.	Concentration on teaching and learning	Maximisation of learning time
		Academic emphasis
		Focus on achievement
5.	High expectations	High expectations all round
		Communicating expectations
		Providing intellectual challenge
6.	Positive reinforcement	Clear and fair discipline
		Feedback
7.	Monitoring progress	Monitoring pupil performance
		Evaluating school performance
8.	Pupil rights and responsibilities	High pupil self-esteem
		Positions of responsibility
		Control of work
9.	Purposeful teaching	Efficient organisation
		Clarity of purpose
		Structured lessons
		Adaptive practice
10.	A learning organisation	School-based staff development
11.	Home–school partnership	Parental involvement (Sammons *et al.*, 1995 p. 8).

A list of factors derived from purely American research on unusually effective schools (Levine and Lezotte, 1990) offers different phraseology but presents a clear overlap with the list of factors above, including an emphasis on understanding by all concerned of the importance of learning, and high expectations under the guidance of the leadership of the institution. The only factor included in the American list that does not have a direct equivalent in the British list is the last, which broadens out the factors to include aspects of schooling not directly related to the core curriculum: 'Other possible correlates including student sense of efficacy/futility, multi-cultural instruction and sensitivity and personal development of students' (adapted from Levine and Lezotte, *ibid.*)

Factors affecting effectiveness in schools in developing countries are different. For example, Walberg's (1991) study of factors promoting science achievement in developing countries listed, amongst other factors, the effect of nutrition:

- length of instructional programmer
- pupil feeding
- school library activity
- years of teacher training
- textbooks and instructional materials (cited in Harber and Davies, 1997, p. 38).

Although this list does not specifically mention the management of the school, the authors do stress the importance of the principal in directing the efforts of the school, particularly in terms of his or her ability to obtain resources. In a review of effectiveness literature relating to schools in both the First and Third Worlds, Davies (1997, p. 29) has selected the factors she considers are 'specifically controllable by management'. These might be:

1. combination of firm leadership and a decision-making process where teachers feel their views are represented;
2. ample use of rewards, praise and appreciation for both students and staff;
3. opportunity for students to take responsibility in the running of the school;
4. low rates of punishment;
5. care of the school environment, buildings and working conditions;
6. clear goals (possibly written) and incorporation (not coercion) of students and parents into acceptance of these goals;
7. high expectations and feedback;
8. teachers as good role models (time-keeping, willingness to deal with pupil problems, lesson preparation and maximum communication with the pupils);
9. clearly delegated duties to teachers and students;
10. consistent record-keeping and monitoring (not necessarily testing);
11. vigorous selection and replacement of staff;
12. maverick orientation, ingenuity in acquiring resources and risk taking by heads;
13. heads 'buffering' schools from negative external influences;
14. convincing teachers they *do* make a difference to children's lives;
15. good external relations to aid financial and moral support for the school;
16. avoidance of nepotism and favouritism (*ibid.*, pp. 29–30).

The list has much in common with the list derived from British literature and quoted above. There are some differences in terms of an emphasis on participation on the part of both staff and students and a stress on clarity of goals, duties and record-keeping. There are also some items included that relate to specific cultural values such as item 16 mentioning nepotism. However, the importance of this list is that it does not link effectiveness solely with the 'input factors' of the ability of students and the level of financial resourcing: 'The above "management controllable" list does not necessarily cost any more money and begins to show what *can* be changed in school management' (*ibid.*, p. 30).

An alternative to the list of features common to effective schools in western countries has been consideration of the nature of *ineffective* schools. It is thought that factors linked with ineffectiveness are not necessarily the reverse of those that are identified with effectiveness. Stoll and Fink (1996) have identified characteristics of ineffective schools, amalgamating the findings of four studies (Mortimore *et al.*, 1986; Rosenholtz, 1989; Teddlie and Stringfield, 1993; Reynolds, 1996) and identifying three whole-school issues: lack of vision where teachers have little attachment 'to anything or anybody' (Rosenholtz 1989); unfocused leadership; and dysfunctional staff relationships.

In addition there is a range of ineffective classroom practices, including the following:

Inconsistent approaches to teaching;
lack of challenge;
low levels of teacher–pupil interaction;
high classroom noise levels;
frequent use of criticism and negative feedback (Stoll and Fink, 1996, pp. 34–5).

❑ The nature of effectiveness research

Although the measurement of effectiveness is generally linked with academic, cognitive test results, qualitative measures have also been used, particularly in the British research. For example, Gray (1995, p. 27) considers that school quality can be assessed by three basic performance indicators, two of which can only be measured through qualitative research involving the interviewing of pupils:

Academic progress
What proportion of pupils have made above average levels of progress over the relevant time-period?

Pupil satisfaction
What proportion of pupils in the school are satisfied with the education they are receiving?

Pupil–teacher relationships
What proportion of pupils in the school have a good or 'vital' relationship with one or more teachers?

Davies (1997, p. 31) points out that 'the narrowness of "measurable outcomes" is ... a cultural problem' and that a goal of self-reliance is likely to be one that is particularly relevant in many developing countries.

Mention has already been made of the measurement of effectiveness within subunits rather than the whole school. It is generally the case that even in schools designated as effective as a whole, there will be departments that are less effective (Gray, 1998). The development of sophisticated multi-level analysis techniques has allowed data to be analysed so that 'differences between classes, year groups and schools can be recognised rather than aggregated together arbitrarily' (Mortimore, 1992, p. 156).

In a large-scale study of primary schools in the Jerusalem area, Yair (1997, p. 241) showed that: 'the net effect of classrooms is significantly higher than the effect of schools, since within-school variability outweighs between-school variability.'

Effectiveness may even consider the level of the individual student. There is little research as to why pupils in the same school have 'very different experiences of schooling' (Gray, 1998, p. 23).

Effectiveness research has tended to look only at outcome measures. The obvious weakness of this is that it takes no account of the 'value-added' by the schools. If outcome measures are to indicate effectiveness, some account must be taken of a range of factors that may include the following (Sammons *et al.*, 1994, p. 4):

Type of factor	Examples
1. Pupils' personal characteristics	Age, sex, prior achievement
2. Family structure	Family size, lone parent status
3. Socio-economic	Parental unemployment, low income, car ownership, social class, housing
4. Educational	Parents' educational qualifications, parents' school-leaving age
5. Ethnicity/language	Ethnic group and level of fluency
6. Other	Mobility of pupils at school or of local population, population density, school characteristics, pupils with statements of special educational needs.

The above list was presented as a step on the way to the more sophisticated delivery of the evaluation of school performance. However, the measurement of the value-added by schools is complex, necessarily taking many factors into account. An attempt to publish national tables of value-added to pupils between the ages of 14 and 16 years by schools in England and Wales in 1998 was postponed:

> The search for a workable way of presenting information showing how schools have performed at GCSE, given the results of tests taken by the year group when aged 14, has proved problematic. In the face of protests from schools that complained the results penalised those with high test scores at 14, the indicator was dropped (Hackett, 1998).

❏ Strengths and weaknesses of effectiveness research

Effectiveness research 'was born out of a quest for more robust evidence to illuminate a complex area, and to reveal a more accurate picture of the many factors in schools which determine standards amongst pupils' (Sammons *et al.*, 1994, p. 1).

We have already seen that effectiveness research has evolved and become more sophisticated. Reynolds *et al.*, (1996, p. 138) outline the particular strengths of the British effectiveness 'knowledge base':

1. A high level of methodological sophistication, including multi-level statistical modelling.
2. The use of multiple measures of pupil outcomes, including attendance, self esteem and attitudes.
3. The use of socio-economic *and* achievement data together.
4. The development of conceptualisations about the role of the 'school level in potentiating or hindering adolescent development'.

Gray (1998, pp. 5–6) sums up the outcomes of effectiveness research:

> a good deal more of the variation in pupils' performance lies within schools than between them; most schools have pupils who are doing well with respect to national norms as well as pupils who are doing badly.

> schools usually account for between 10–15 per cent of the variation in pupils' performances; and

> around 1 in 8 schools may be doing well, given their intakes, whilst a similar proportion may be doing badly; the greater bulk of schools (between two-thirds and three-quarters) are, however, performing around the levels one would predict from knowledge of their pupils' starting points.

> there is a great variability in the performance of subject departments within schools.

In regard to developing countries, Harber and Davies (1997, p. 37) point out that the effects of educational processes on student achievement are larger in developing countries than in developed countries, sometimes indicating a variance of up to 28 per cent resulting from the differential effectiveness of individual schools.

However, some findings on effectiveness, particularly in the early years of the research, have been contradictory, e.g. high levels of staff turnover have been found to be associated with both secondary school effectiveness and ineffectiveness (Rutter *et al.*, 1979; Reynolds, 1982; 1992). There are consistent American findings on a positive link between frequent monitoring of pupil progress and academic effectiveness, whilst Mortimore *et al.* (1988) found this a characteristic of ineffective schools (Reynolds, 1992).

More grounded criticisms of effectiveness research centre on the following points, outlined by Reynolds *et al.* (1996):

1. Most studies in the west have been within disadvantaged or deprived contexts rather than with schools in advantaged areas.
2. There has generally been less of a focus on classroom processes.
3. 'the historic lack of any "interface" between school effectiveness research and school improvement practice' (*ibid.*, p. 139).
4. There have only been rudimentary attempts at theory generation.

To this list may be added further possible criticisms that indicate the need to interpret effectiveness data carefully. Creemers and Reezigt (1997, p. 411) suggest that the lists of correlates derived from effectiveness studies tend to suggest more than empirical evidence actually shows:

> most correlates are derived from pre-effectiveness studies in which each of them was the only independent variable. The correlates have not often been studied together ... As far as correlates do have effects, these are not very stable. They often do not hold over time, subjects, grades, groups of students, departments within schools, districts, countries and so on.

They also claim that effectiveness studies ignore the processes in educational institutions and forget that the research is focusing on a school or schools at a certain point in time. Harber and Davies (1997) quote the work of Harbison and Hanushek (1992) who, in a large-scale study, showed the difficulty in identifying teacher effectiveness through quantitative measures only: 'the choice of quantitative differences between teachers such as their years of formal education ignores other far more important aspects of their "art"' (Harber and Davies, 1997, p. 36).

Many of the criticisms lead us to the consideration of school improvement and the complementary nature of effectiveness and improvement research: 'awareness of the findings of school effectiveness research is a necessary (although not sufficient) condition for school improvement' (Sammons *et al.*, 1994, p. 1).

Before turning to the issues associated with institutional improvement, please complete the following activity.

Activity

It could be argued that the main purpose of management in schools and colleges is to enhance effectiveness. In order to clarify your own knowledge of what effectiveness means in your institution:

1. Identify any documents that relate to effectiveness in your workplace.
2. Decide how effectiveness is defined.
3. What are the means of measuring it?

❑ Comments

Your responses will be specific to your own situation. However, certain issues may have emerged which will illuminate your understanding of the management of effectiveness in you institution:

1. How easy was it to obtain definitions of effectiveness?
2. Are these definitions known and acted on by all staff?
3. What are the problems in collecting the evidence?
4. To what extent is effectiveness measured and managed?

The concept of improvement

Improvement is generally associated with the efforts of an individual institution, relying on the professional experience of its teachers and other staff to identify a focus for improvement for that institution. It can be identified with the concept of the teacher as researcher and has encompassed projects related to self-evaluation and review such as the Guidelines for Review and Internal Development in Schools (GRIDS) scheme. It can also be seen in the efforts of further education colleges to widen participation and increase retention and achievement of students, although the results of such efforts are then measured by the Performance Indicators mentioned earlier (FEFC, 1998). Improvement has tended to focus on change to processes rather than directly on outcomes, and has been identified with qualitative evaluation rather than quantitative: 'it can be seen that the disciplines of school effectiveness and school improvement have been "coming from" very different places intellectually, methodologically and theoretically' (Reynolds *et al.*, 1996, p. 144).

Since its inception, it has had an international dimension. The International School Improvement Project (ISIP) adopted the following definition of school improvement: 'A systematic, sustained effort aimed at change in learning conditions and other related internal conditions in one or more schools, with the ultimate aim of accomplishing educational goals more effectively' (Van Velzen *et al.*, 1985, p. 48).

From this it can be seen that school and college improvement, in contrast to effectiveness, may be concerned with changes to factors not directly related to student achievement. For example, improvement may stress the professional development of staff, which it is hoped will indirectly lead to student success. Improvement is 'an approach to educational change that is concerned with process as well as outcomes. School improvement is about raising student achievement through enhancing the teaching-learning process and the conditions which support it. It is about strategies for improving the school's capacity for providing quality education' (Hopkins, 1994a, p. 75).

At this stage it may be helpful to compare some of the major differences identified between improvement and effectiveness (Table 6.1). Although these differences have been drawn from literature relating to schools, they may also be applied to the college environment.

Table 6.1 The separate traditions of school effectiveness and school improvement

School effectiveness	School improvement
Focus on schools	Focus on individual teachers or groups of teachers
Focus on school organisation	Focus on school processes
Data driven, with emphasis on outcomes	Rare empirical evaluation of effects of changes
Quantitative in orientation	Qualitative in orientation
Lack of knowledge about how to implement change strategies	Concerned with change in schools exclusively
More concerned with change in pupil outcomes	More concerned with journey of school improvement than its destination
More concerned with schools at a point in time	More concerned with schools as changing
Based on research knowledge	Focus on practitioner knowledge

Source: from Reynolds *et al.* (1993).

There is a clear identification of improvement with change, particularly the change of processes. Building on the Fullan explanation of the three processes of change (initiation, implementation and institutionalisation), Stoll and Fink (1996, pp. 45–6) list what they see as the main change process issues:

- there is not only one version of what the change should be
- people have to understand the change and work it out for themselves in practice
- change is often accompanied by stress and anxiety
- change is approached differently in each school
- conflict and disagreement are inevitable
- a mix of pressure and support is needed
- top-down and bottom-up change together work effectively
- change rarely involves a single innovation
- effective change takes time
- there must be times of consolidation
- change may not be implemented for valid reasons
- some people will not change; 'don't water the rocks'
- it is necessary to plan taking into account these assumptions
- development is evolutionary, difficult to plan in too much detail
- the real agenda is changing school culture not single innovations.

Activity

Identify an example of attempted improvement in your institution. Was it successful or unsuccessful? Relate the level of success to the bullet points above.

❑ Comment

Whatever the scale of improvement, the clear issues seem to be those of 'ownership' of the change, allowing time for implementation and the relationship of the change to the culture of the institution: 'Many externally (and some internally) imposed changes do not improve student outcomes, and most appear to neglect the importance of the culture and organization of the school as key factors in sustaining teacher and curriculum development' (Hopkins, 1994a, p. 75).

In examining the introduction of three innovations in the Caribbean school systems, Jennings (1994, p. 309) emphasises 'making users aware of the relevance of the innovation to their needs, [and] enabling the implementers to participate in decision making'.

The issue of managing strategic change is considered in Chapter 8.

❑ The relationship of improvement to culture

The aim of improving a school or college will inevitably have an impact on its culture (see our earlier discussion of culture). There are considerable implications where there is a culture that is resistant to change. Hopkins (1994b, p. 15) has identified four types of school cultures, each of which would relate very differently to issues of improvement:

1. THE MOVING SCHOOL

a healthy blend of change and stability
adapts well to a changing environment
retains its ethos and traditions
a sense of calm
achieves high outcomes
'we keep everything under review'

2. THE STUCK SCHOOL

a pervading sense of mediocrity and powerlessness
'we've tried, but things just don't work'
teaching is an isolated activity
expectations are very low
external conditions are blamed
'there's not much we can do with these kids/parents'

3. THE PROMENADING SCHOOL

living on past achievements
doesn't move fast or far
a traditional school – with a stable staff reluctant to change
scores well on the 'league tables' – but 'value added' may be low
attractive to many parents
'we're pretty pleased with things as they are'

4. THE WANDERING SCHOOL

has, and is, experiencing too much innovation
the appearance of change – but little of its reality
staff exhausted and fragmented
there's movement – but it lacks a clear destination
some groups or individuals go their own way
'we've tried lots of things, but nothing gets finished.'

Hargreaves (1997) has developed two typologies of school cultures. The first includes:

the formal – a traditional school with an emphasis on discipline;

the welfarist school – a happy, child-centred school where students are not driven;

the hothouse school – where expectations are very high;

the survivalist school – where the emphasis is simply on maintaining basic control: 'The ethos is one of insecurity, hopelessness and low morale' (adapted from *ibid.*, p. 241).

The second typology basically divides schools into two types: the traditional, bureaucratic model and the collegial model (see our earlier discussion of models of educational management). Hargreaves *ibid.*, p. 245) comments about the latter: 'Over the last hundred years or so, the general drift seems to be from the traditional towards the collegial . . . This evolution reflects many of the wider changes in society.'

The first typology can be seen to be related to aspects of school effectiveness. For example, the formal and the hothouse school might be expected to achieve well in terms of the simple measures of academic success, whereas the welfarist school might score less well in terms of academic success, but better on measures that relate to student satisfaction. The survivalist school is likely to do badly on all measures.

The second typology cannot be related to effectiveness, since it concerns the culture of the teachers rather than the aspects of the school that relate directly to pupil achievement. However, it could be related to school improvement:

'No school or teacher culture can be shown to have a *direct* impact on student learning and achievement, and claims to that end are vacuous. But the effects of culture can be conceptualised as trickling down, so to speak, through the architecture – political and micro-political, maintenance and development and service – until they eventually make some impact on what goes on in classrooms (*ibid.*, p. 249).

In the consideration of culture, effectiveness, improvement and change, Hargreaves (*ibid.*) calls for more research in these areas, mapping the process of change, thus enabling us to see more clearly the possible relationships, for example, between a collaborative culture and school improvement.

The assumption of the importance of shared understanding and collaboration can be seen in the following list of ten principles which 'capture the essence of improvement' (adapted from Hopkins, 1994a, pp. 79–80):

1. The main focus for action should be on teaching and learning in classrooms, in order that *all* students develop 'the intellectual and imaginative powers and competencies' they need in as personalized a way as possible.
2. Such classroom practice can only be sustained through ongoing staff development.
3. Leadership should empower people (students, staff and community) to achieve their own and the school's purposes.
4. All members of a school community should actively build and share a common vision of its main purposes.
5. The school's current priorities should reflect its main purposes and its vision, and be generated through consultation.
6. Work on the current priorities should be based upon planning in order to manage the process of change.
7. The substance of staff development should be teaching skills, as well as the best available knowledge of curriculum content.
8. Collaboration is a necessary condition for staff development and school improvement.
9. Processes of improvement should be informed by monitoring, feedback and reflection on the part of students as well as staff and, of course, the school.
10. Successful policy implementation occurs when groups of teachers adapt educational ideas to their own context and professional needs.

Hopkins (*ibid.*, p. 80) concludes that 'the significance of these principles lies in their synergism: together they are greater than the sum of their parts'.

These ten principles represent a potentially ideal scenario. The identification of some of the ways in which progress could be made towards this ideal is helpful. Joyce (1991, p. 59) draws on experience in the USA to suggest five 'doors' that each open a passageway to improvement. These are as follows:

Collegiality: developing cohesive professional relations within schools.

Research: helping school staff to study research findings about effective school practices or instructional alternatives.

Site-specific information: helping staff to collect and analyse data about their schools and their students' progress.

Curriculum initiatives: introducing changes within subject areas or across the curriculum.

Instructional initiatives: teachers study teaching skills and strategies.

'All these emphases can eventually change the culture of the school substantially. Perhaps, if we look carefully at each door to school improvement, we can discover where each is likely to lead, how the passageways are connected, what proponents of any one approach can borrow from the others, and the costs and benefits of opening any one (or any combination) first' (Hopkins, 1994a, p. 85).

These doors are opened from inside the institution. Stoll and Fink (1996) point out that some doors can be opened from outside. These could include initiatives as diverse as an inspection, the implementation of quality approaches, applying for Investors in People or initiatives driven by a regional educational organisation such as an LEA. Indeed, the stated intention of the inspection service in England and Wales is the improvement of schools: 'The purpose of inspection is to identify strengths and weaknesses in schools so that they may improve the quality of education offered and raise the standards achieved by their pupils' (Ofsted, 1994, Framework, p. 5).

However, the evidence appears to be that the impact of external inspection in schools for improvement is modified by a range of factors.

❑ Comment

In this chapter, a range of research evidence relating to the impact of inspection on schools is presented. It appears that, whilst inspection findings are generally considered helpful, their impact lessens over time, is related to the degree of 'ownership', and that the values and culture of the school continue as an important influence possibly over-riding inspection findings in the long run.

However, the impact of an external impetus for change may be a key element in change for improvement. In some cases inspection may act as a 'wake-up call', in others, externally generated change may be adapted to provide a vehicle for improvement. Early responses to the inspection of schools in Hong Kong show that:

> Schools were prepared to take immediate action to look into the relevant issues raised through measures such as the setting up of working groups.

> Schools would use the QA inspection report as an important reference for formulating future development plans (Education Department, Hong Kong, 1998, p. ix).

In the UK the provision of government initiatives linked to additional funding, such as the bidding for technology college status, might have provided an opportunity for change and improvement. Hopkins (1996a) identifies a framework for school improvement based on the work with the Improving the Quality of Education for All (IQEA) project, which shows the relationship between an external impetus which is then developed as a priority within the school and becomes part of the strategy that leads to improvement, once embedded within the culture of the school.

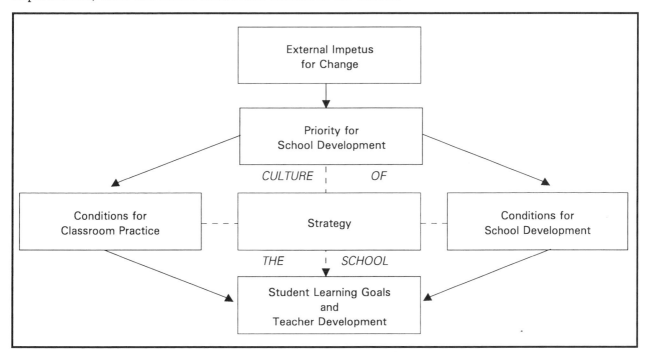

Figure 6.1 A framework for school improvement
Source: Hopkins, 1996a

One aspect of the culture of a school that may impact considerably on its potential for improvement is the extent to which the pupils of that school are advantaged or disadvantaged from a socio-economic point of view. Mortimore and Whitty (1997, pp. 11–12) consider there is an issue of the role of school improvement in relation to the establishment of equity: 'Probably the single most significant factor that currently distinguishes the most academically successful schools (even if not the most "effective" ones in value added terms) is that only a small proportion of their pupils come from disadvantaged homes.'

The impact on staff of striving for school improvement in relatively disadvantaged schools should not be ignored:

> committed and talented heads and teachers can improve schools even if such schools contain a proportion of disadvantaged pupils. In order to achieve improvement, however, such schools have to exceed what could be termed 'normal' efforts. Members of staff have to be *more committed* and *work harder* than their peers elsewhere . . . What is more, they have to *maintain the effort* so as to sustain the improvement. There can be no switching on the 'automatic pilot' if schools are aiming to buck the trend. We must, however, be aware of the dangers of basing a national strategy for change on the efforts of outstanding individuals working in exceptional circumstances (*ibid.*, p. 6, emphasis in original).

The authors recommend action involving the support of outside agencies and the focusing of different types of support on schools with a large proportion of pupils from disadvantaged backgrounds.

❑ Effectiveness and improvement together

Despite the difference in theoretical orientation of the two 'movements', there is obviously much to be said for the combination of the two approaches: 'A major aim in the field of school effectiveness always was to link theory development and research on the one hand and practice and policy making, especially school improvement, on the other hand' (Creemers and Reezigt, 1997, p. 398).

Creemers and Reezigt (*ibid.*) make a case for communication between effectiveness and improvement projects at all stages, referring to the concept of 'sustained interactivity' (Huberman, 1990). The procedure for the continuing dialogue is set out in Figure 6.2.

However, in practice, differences remain. The advocates of the research orthodoxy of effectiveness are critical of the research methods associated with improvement, sometimes betraying their own, possibly entrenched, positivist stance: 'Some school improvers have preferred forms of action research instead of research-based experiments' (*ibid.*, p. 403).

There is also concern on the part of those involved in school effectiveness research about the adequacy of evaluation in school improvement projects. Nevertheless there is a growing number of instances of the merging of the two traditions. The IQEA project is one such example: 'It is pupil outcome orientated, involves measurement of programme success or failure at outcome level but is also concerned with the within-school study of school processes from a qualitative orientation' (Reynolds *et al.*, 1993, p. 46).

A further example at departmental level (Harris, 1998) is the consideration through case studies of eight departments in two schools, to attempt to establish the parameters of less effective departments. One of the criteria for choosing the schools was that they 'were all schools that undertook systematic value-added data collection and analysis' (*ibid.*, p. 270). Thus a qualitative approach more typical of school improvement was applied, using as a basis data derived from effectiveness research.

The effectiveness paradigm focuses on establishing valid measures of performance for educational institutions, and subunits within them, in order to assess the extent to which they are meeting their objectives, which may be determined by internal or external groups. Improvement uses these data as a starting point for a programme of sustained change directed at making the organisation more effective.

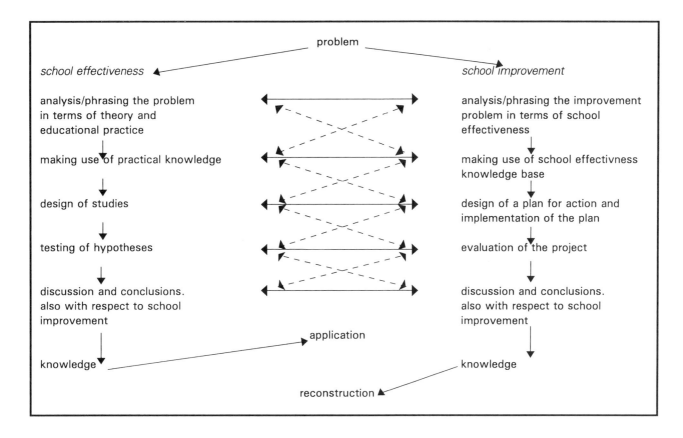

Figure 6.2 Sustained interactivity between school effectiveness and school improvement
Source: Creemers and Reezigt, 1997, p. 421

In the end, theories of effectiveness and of improvement may share some of the same difficulties:

> Essentially, the main questions for both school effectiveness and school improvement is not which multitude of isolated factors might be of some influence on student outcomes, but which configurations of factors have a major impact and would therefore form the starting point for school improvement. It may take a long time effort directed to a diversity of factors at different levels of the educational system to establish and then secure substantial improvements (Creemers and Reezigt, 1997, p. 416).

The concept of quality

The wording of aims and of mission statements may include reference to effectiveness or to improvement, but may equally include aspirations involving quality. Concepts such as transformational leadership may also be relevant.

Lee and Walker (1997, p. 103) in discussing a whole-school approach to curriculum change in a case-study school in Hong Kong, identify two paradigms, stating that the new paradigm is most fitted to the encouragement of quality education:

Old paradigm	New paradigm
Management	Leadership (All workers are managers)
Vertical ladder	Sideways (More open and participative decision making structures)
Fixed roles	Flexible roles

Individual responsibility	Shared responsibility (Teamwork)
Autocratic	Collaborative
Delivering expertise	Developing expertise (An effective system of staff appraisal and staff development)
Status	Stature (All participants are valued for their unique and special contributions)
Efficiency	Effectiveness
Control	Release (All members are able to commit their skills and energies to an organisation in a culture of encouragement and support)
Power	Empowerment (Getting things done and supporting the people who do it)

Quality is being used here in a fairly general sense but, in management terms, quality assurance and concepts such as total quality management (TQM) take on more specific meanings.

The concepts of quality assurance and of TQM have been derived from industry, but have become important in education. For example, in Hong Kong, 'quality school education' enshrined in the consultative document ECR7 recommended the development of a complete framework for 'developing and monitoring quality school education' (Dimmock, 1998, p. 365). Ideas of quality management have been found to be particularly appropriate in the further education sector in the UK:

> Most colleges now recognise that continuous quality improvement is essential if they are to survive and prosper. Often this is reflected in their mission statements and strategic and operational plans. A management philosophy with which many people in FE are familiar and feel comfortable is Total Quality Management (TQM). It has continuous quality improvement at its heart (FEFC, 1997, pp. 39–40).

However, advice to colleges of further education has been to 'make quality your own' (FEU, 1995) and lists a range of quality models and approaches which may be appropriate to the individual college. The name given to the model of quality adopted may be relatively unimportant:

> Three years ago a TQM approach was useful for us: it gave us the tools to monitor our performance rigorously using data and helped us clarify our provision in terms of internal and external customers, products and services. Now developmental priorities have changed and we are working towards IIP [Investors in People] because it takes our own objectives forward. Sometimes the label or the kite-mark can get in the way and become an end in itself. The important thing is the quality of the experience of our students and other customers (internal and external). Colleges need to re-shape ideas in the quality literature to suit themselves and their priorities. Often the label or acronym is irrelevant (Dr R. Evans, Principal, Stockport College of Further and Higher Education, quoted in FEU, 1995, p. 8).

The inspection framework for colleges of further education (FEFC, 1993) sets out the elements of quality assurance which inspectors have assessed:

> policies on quality and its assurance and control;
> establishment, monitoring and review of standards and targets;
> use of performance indicators;
> regular reports including statistical and evaluative feedback from a range of stakeholders including students and employers;
> linkage with staff appraisal and staff development (adapted from *ibid.*, p. 14).

However, the new inspection regime has more emphasis on validating self-assessment: 'The revised inspection framework is designed to promote within the sector a self-critical culture through an emphasis on self-assessment and an inspection programme which assesses each college's ability to make comprehensive and accurate judgements about its provision on the basis of rigorous procedures for quality assurance' (FEFC, 1997, pp. 68–9).

In effect a policy for quality has been built into the system through the need for self-assessment. Colleges will be given accredited status when inspectors are assured of:

the existence in the college of formal and effective monitoring and quality assurance arrangements;

regular and rigorous self-assessment, validated during the course of a college inspection;

the setting and consistent achievement of appropriate targets for institutional performance and demonstration that students' achievements are being improved and/or maintained at a high level over a three-year period;

effective action to address weaknesses and demonstrate accountability (*ibid.*, p. 70)

Similarly, in the higher education sector, the Higher Education Quality Council (HEQC, 1996) has set out guidelines for universities on quality assurance. These guidelines are not intended to impose a system but to indicate the areas that should be addressed by the institution through quality assurance, where: 'Quality assurance is the means through which an institution confirms that the conditions are in place for students to achieve the standards set by the institution' (*ibid.*, 1996, p. 11).

Quality assurance may be the system that is most relevant to the management of standards that relate to customer requirements. However, West-Burnham (1992, p. 15) takes up the relevance of TQM as a management process, stating that 'Quality has to be seen in terms of relationships rather than intangible (and unattainable) goals'. The crux of the relationships may be seen in the nature of the processes of inspection, quality control quality assurance and quality management, which West-Burnham implies form a hierarchy of approaches, with inspection seen as one end of a spectrum and TQM at the other (Figure 6.3).

Total quality management
- Involves suppliers and customers
- Aiming for continuous improvement
- Concerns products and processes
- Responsibility with all workers
- Delivered through teamwork

Quality assurance
- Use of statistical process control
- Emphasis on prevention
- External accreditation
- Delegated involvement
- Audit of quality systems
- Cause-and-effect analysis

Quality control
- Concerned with product testing
- Responsibility with supervisors
- Limited quality criteria
- Some self-inspection
- Paper-based systems

Inspection
- Post-production review
- Reworking
- Rejection
- Control of workforce
- Limited to physical products

Figure 6.3 The hierarchy of quality management
Source: Dale and Plunkett, 1990, p. 4; West-Burnham, 1992, p. 15.

⊚ Reading

For further reading relevant to the relationship between these approaches, see West-Burnham, J., 'Inspection, evaluation and quality assurance', Chapter 8 in Bush, T. and West-Burnham, J. (eds.) *The Principles of Educational Management*.

West-Burnham (1992, p. 16) claims that progression through this perceived hierarchy towards TQM leads to four significant cultural changes:

- there is increasing awareness and involvement of clients and suppliers.
- personal responsibility of the work force increases.
- there is increasing emphasis on process as well as product.
- the imperative is towards continuous improvement.

The empirical evidence to support these perceived changes is limited, but some of these elements may be observable in certain schools and colleges (see later examples and also Davies and West-Burnham, 1997).

Origins of TQM and its applicability to education

Although TQM was established in Japan, it was inspired by Americans, Deming and Juran and later Crosby. It started as a purely statistical approach, but has been extended and developed by the 'gurus' of TQM and by industrialists in Japan and the USA. There are famous 'lists' relating to the move towards total quality: the 14 points of Deming (see p. 64) and Juran's 10 and Crosby's 14 steps to quality improvement. Crosby's four absolutes of quality management may be seen as a summary of TQM as it has been applied to industry:

1. The definition   Quality is conformance to customer requirements, not intrinsic goodness.
2. The system   Prevention, not detection.
3. The standard   Zero defects.
4. The measurement   The price of non-conformance (West-Burnham, 1992, p. 17).

From the lists and 'absolutes' derived from industry, it is possible to see that much, but not all, could be appropriate to schools and other educational institutions. In particular, the aspiration to zero defects as a performance standard is described by West-Burnham (*ibid.*) as 'hopelessly unrealistic'.

The definition of TQM offered by Marsh J. (1992) is helpful in stressing what may be the most salient aspects for education: 'Total quality is a philosophy with tools and processes for practical implementation aimed at achieving a culture of continuous improvement driven by all the employees of an organisation in order to satisfy and delight customers' (quoted in West-Burnham, 1995, p. 13).

The main implications are as follows:

- The emphasis on totality – it is inclusive of *all* the employees. In education this would include support staff as well as teaching and lecturing staff.
- There is shared understanding of an explicit set of values with implications for leadership and management style.
- There is a planning process to allow for practical implementation.
- Tools and processes include monitoring and evaluation with an emphasis on prevention rather than inspection.
- Attention is given to customer rather than provider needs and customers are both external (e.g. students and parents) and internal (e.g. staff).

West-Burnham (1994a, p. 172) argues that TQM has much to offer schools and colleges because it is:

- value-driven; it has a clear moral imperative.
- customer-focused; existing for, and driven by the needs of, young people, parents and community.
- based on prevention; concerned with optimising outcomes.

West-Burnham *et al.* (1995, p. 28) produce a list of key features of TQM based on a review of the literature:

1. Quality is defined in terms of customer's needs rather than those of the supplier.
2. Quality management is based on continuous improvement and an emphasis on prevention rather than detection.
3. Quality can be measured.
4. Quality requires visionary leadership but this does not diminish individual responsibility.
5. Quality has to pervade relationships in the work place e.g. flat structures and team-based management.
6. Quality management is driven by vision and values.
7. Quality assurance involves high levels of consistency.
8. Quality management requires constant review.

❑ TQM and customers

The focus on customers is one of the central tenets of TQM. In this respect, it reflects one of the main themes of the British government's educational policy. The School Management Initiative (SMI) in Hong Kong might also be regarded as a vehicle for increasing responsiveness to customer requirements.

Arguably, there is a greater commitment within education to the needs of the consumer but there remains uncertainty and disagreement about consumer identity and about how consumer needs should be defined. Juran (1989, p. 17) adopts a broad definition: 'A customer is anyone who is affected by the product or process. Customers may be external or internal.'

Taylor and Hill (1997) make the point that, in education, the customer is not simply the individual at the receiving end of the educational process, but the customer–supplier relationship may also include interactions between the administrative and academic staff and between the administrative staff and the students. In the case of a higher education institution:

> the students' perceptions of the organization may be heavily influenced by non-academic staff. There is also some evidence to suggest that seemingly 'trivial' factors, such as how the gatekeeper deals with visitors when the car-park is full, or how the switchboard operator deals with callers, not only are significantly symptomatic of the organization's culture but also can make a major impact on the enquirer's perception of the organization's quality of service (ibid., p. 167).

West-Burnham (1995) identifies four of the central principles of the customer focus within TQM theory:

1. Quality is defined by the customer not the supplier (e.g. lessons should be 'fit for purpose').
2. Schools and colleges should be 'close to the customer' in that they meet their needs (e.g. parents' consultation arrangements should match the availability of parents rather than the convenience of teachers).
3. Quality schools and colleges 'know their customers' and take the trouble to find out their needs and preferences (e.g. parental or student surveys on aspects of school life).
4. Customer satisfaction may be determined by 'moments of truth', striking examples of good or poor quality. Quality consists in the experiences of the customer rather than the aspirations of the supplier. (adapted from *ibid.*, p. 22)

However, Capper and Jamison (1993) adopt a critical perspective on TQM, particularly in respect of its customer focus. They argue (*ibid.*, p. 28) that TQM theorists give too little attention to differences between customers and in their ability to influence the nature of services:

> TQM advocates blithely assume, without question, that all 'customers' have equal access to resources and

services, and ignore power differences that would enable and constrain customer decisions. For example, it is usually customers with the most power who receive the goods and services and who, in turn, will define 'quality', whether that power is based on combinations of income, race, gender, ability, religion, sexual orientation, or other personal characteristics…TQM's naive belief that the customer's voice will be heard ignores the forces that elevate some customer voices and silence others.

The point is reinforced by Riley (1997, p. 27), who states that the 'purchasing power of the education consumer is limited'. The limitations include not having the financial resources to exit from public education, the limitations in practice on parental choice of school, and the fact that, unlike customers in a supermarket, the customer in education '*has* to buy' (*ibid.*, p. 28).

This powerful critique rings true in education. It is often middle-class parents who benefit most from the extra choice arising from customer responsiveness. However, this caution does not mean that teachers are likely to be better at defining need than parents or students. Rather, school and college managers should invest time and effort in establishing the requirements of all customers, not just those who are most vocal or persistent.

❑ TQM: examples of application to education

One of the best known examples of the practical application of TQM principles to education is at Mt Edgecumbe High School in Alaska (Cotton, 1994). This school has about 300 residential students, most of whom are drawn from 14 Native American and other ethnic minority groups. A quarter of the students come from families with poverty-level incomes. The implementation of TQM principles over the course of a year by the business studies teacher, following attendance at a course, led to the involvement of students and interest amongst the rest of the staff who moved forward to implement a modified version of Deming's 14 points. The original points follow:

1. Create constancy of purpose for continual improvement of products and services.
2. Adopt the new philosophy and abandon traditional ways of working.
3. Move from inspection to building quality into every product and process.
4. Stop awarding contracts on the basis of the lowest bid – specify and buy quality.
5. Engage in a process of continually improving every aspect of company activity.
6. Use work based training techniques.
7. The emphasis for leaders and managers must be on quality, not quantity.
8. Drive out fear by improving communication.
9. Break down organisation barriers.
10. Eliminate slogans and exhortations.
11. Eliminate arbitrary numerical targets.
12. Allow for pride of workmanship by locating responsibility with the worker.
13. Encourage education and self development.
14. Create a management structure and culture that will drive the preceding 13 points. (West-Burnham, J., 1992, p. 18)

These points were adapted by staff and students at Mt Edgecumbe and became:

1. Create and maintain a constancy of purpose toward improvement of students and service.
2. Embrace the new philosophy.
3. Work to abolish grading and the harmful effects of rating people.
4. Cease dependence on testing to achieve quality.
5. Work with the educational institutions from which students come.
6. Improve constantly and forever the system of student improvement and service.
7. Institute continuous training on the job.
8. Institute leadership.
9. Drive out fear.
10. Break down barriers between departments. Work as a team.
11. Eliminate slogans, exhortations, and targets for teachers and students asking for perfect performance and new levels of productivity.
12. Eliminate work standard (quotas) on teachers and students.

13. Remove barriers that rob the students, teachers and management of their right to pride and joy of workmanship.
14. Institute a vigorous program of education and self-improvement for everyone.
15. Put everybody in the community to work to accomplish the transformation. (Adapted from Cotton, 1994, p. 3)

The programme has been supported by bimonthly TQM training activities for both teachers and students. A notable feature of the change at the school is the change in the relationship of the 'customer' and the 'provider':

> the high degree of responsibility students take for managing and assessing their own learning. In keeping with the TQM philosophy, the teacher serves in a facilitator/coach/counsel capacity, assisting students to conceive projects – projects being the chief means by which students develop and demonstrate competency. Teachers help students to determine what competencies are needed, how they will be assessed, and how to work through and evaluate agreed upon project components (Cotton, 1994, p. 5).

The second example, of an English secondary school with 670 pupils in Sheffield (Sisum, 1997), gives an indication of both how a quality approach may be used as a framework for school improvement and of the difficulties inherent in any process that seeks to change the culture of the school. In this case the impetus for the introduction of TQM came with the attendance of 12 teachers, a governor and a member of the support team at an induction course for TQM organised by industry. When the group returned to school, the decision was made to involve the staff first and initially not the pupils:

> In hindsight, this was probably one of the most serious mistakes we made. Total Quality approaches require the involvement of all from the start...The failure of this initial period was based on our lack of real understanding of the principal concepts inherent in the Total Quality approach and a mistaken belief that Total Quality was just about the mechanics of processes rather than the underlying principles and values of involvement and customer focus. We also underestimated the resistance of our colleagues to the language of Total Quality, which they perceived as being too business-orientated (*ibid.*, p. 114).

Since that realisation, the school has moved on. The head had a secondment, enabling him to develop his own understanding of TQM, the school faced a very real crisis in terms of budgetary problems and went through an Ofsted inspection. The acceptance and use of TQM techniques in handling the budgetary problems and preparing a post-inspection action plan were an important part of the process leading to improvement:

> We have a much more positive approach to monitoring and evaluation, and colleagues are much more accepting of the idea of measurement and asking the educational customer for their views. There is a genuine desire to look outside the school and to benchmark against good and best practice in other schools (*ibid.*, p. 124).

These two examples illustrate some of the main tenets of the TQM philosophy. However, they also illustrate the fact that TQM may be problematic because it challenges three existing educational norms:

• It challenges the control and dependency models implicit in inspection models.
• It replaces notions of professional autonomy with common purpose and teamwork.
• It replaces 'knowledge as teacher control' with 'learning as student control'.

TQM might offer a number of ways forward to educational organisations:

• A combination of philosophy and practice.
• A holistic and integrated approach.
• Wide-ranging experience and resources.
• The concept of *total management*.

In addition, it can be seen that the adoption of principles of TQM can be used as a 'door' to school improvement.

<table>
<tr><td>

Activity
</td></tr>
</table>

Are total quality, school improvement and school effectiveness the same concept, apart from the jargon?

Consider this question in terms of the overall aims of strategic management of your school or college.

❏ Comment

The adoption of any of the three approaches certainly involves thinking and management at a strategic level. In the case of all three there is emphasis on the long-term development of the organisation. The importance of shared values and of the involvement of the whole organisation are key elements of both TQM and school improvement, as is the need to address organisational culture. However, whilst TQM and improvement involve an individual and internally motivated approach to change for the organisation, measures of effectiveness can be both internally and externally imposed and monitored. Effectiveness concerns measured outcomes, whilst improvement and TQM stress the processes that are involved in eventually reaching more effective outcomes.

All three have in common an incremental approach to improvement. However, a more radical strategic stance may be possible.

Re-engineering

It may be appropriate for strategic thinking and planning to encompass the possibility of radical change. Here, the concept of re-engineering outpaces the approaches described above. As with TQM, re-engineering is a concept, derived from business, that may have applications for education. The formal definition of re-engineering is: 'the fundamental rethinking and radical redesign of business processes to achieve dramatic improvement in critical contemporary measures of performance, such as cost, quality, service and speed' (Hammer and Champy, 1993, p. 32).

Whilst aspects of this definition apply much more obviously to business than to education, the aspect of 'fundamental rethinking' may be seen to be relevant. Davies (1997) identifies a re-engineering perspective in the view that Hargreaves (1994) has taken of the schools of the new century. Some of his perspectives reveal a view that challenges our stereotypes about schooling, for example, that schools of the future should:

be smaller, differentiated and specialised, giving more choice to students, parents and teachers;

be independent institutions, financed on the basis of a national formula, accountable to parents and collaborating in consortia as voluntary associations; . . .

have a core of full-time, highly trained professional teachers, on five year renewable contracts, supported by a range of assistant teachers and part-time teachers who also work in other fields;

contract out substantial parts of their teaching functions, so that secondary pupils spend less of their time in school (Hargreaves, 1994, pp.53–4, quoted in Davies, 1997, p. 179).

Elsewhere, Bowring-Carr and West-Burnham (1997) have indicated the potential impact of information and communications technology on the way in which schools may operate. The freedom given to city technology colleges has allowed the opportunity to radically restructure the working pattern of the typical school. The analysis of GCSE results in England in 1998 showed that one of these schools recorded the highest points score of any comprehensive school. The headteacher attributed much of the success to two radical moves: the extended week of 35 compared to the normal 25 hours and the institution of performance-related pay for teachers (Hackett, 1998). Similarly, benefits have been felt in CTCs in adopting a five-term year rather than the normal three-term model of British schools:

> As predicted, eight weeks had proved to be an ideal length of time for a school term: long enough to deliver curriculum modules effectively and efficiently without the hindrance of a half-term interruption but not too long for the concentration span of either the teacher or the taught to waver (Lewis, 1997, p. 53).

On the level of the individual school, re-engineering can be applied to a part rather than the whole institution:

> Re-engineering...can focus on one section of an organisation and re-engineer it. One case study school...that re-engineered the teaching of one subject area for 16 year olds by the use of interactive technology, improved pupil performance by 25 per cent while reducing teacher input by 60 per cent. However, the limitation of this approach is that it can be partial and not driven through the whole organisation. The advantage, on the other hand, is that schools can make significant shifts in patterns of operation and create a climate for change (Davies and West-Burnham, 1997, p. 13).

The more radical approach of re-engineering may fit some of the needs of strategic managers faced either with specific or intense problems or with the 'blank sheet of paper' described by Lewis (1997) above. In this it may be likened to the concept of zero-based budgeting: 'taking a fresh look at expenditure by starting with a "clean slate" rather than by basing decisions on previous practice' (Davies, 1994, p. 346). Table 6.2 indicates the major differences between a TQM approach and a re-engineering approach.

Table 6.2 Fundamental differences between TQM and business process re-engineering

Factors	TQM	Re-engineering
Type of change	Evolutionary – a better way to compete	Revolutionary – a new way of doing business
Method	Adds value to existing processes	Challenges process fundamentals and their very existence
Scope	Encompasses whole organisation	Focuses on core business processes
Role of technology	Traditional support, e.g. management information system	Use as enabler

Source: Davies and West-Burnham (1997, p. 12).

So far in this chapter we have considered the wider purposes of strategic management, concentrating on the different routes and philosophies that school and college managers might adopt in guiding their institutions towards improvement. We now turn to the more practical aspects of strategic and development planning and their implementation.

❑ Building on key learning points

- Whilst effectiveness stresses outcomes and improvement stresses processes, the two 'movements' are increasingly seen as complementary.
- Issues of the management of quality through quality assurance, TQM or other quality systems are linked to both improvement and accountability and relate to customer requirements.
- There may be a case for 'fundamental rethinking' in education.

---

7. Strategic and development planning in education

This chapter considers:

- strategic planning; and
- development planning.

Introduction

The concept of strategic management, its relationship to autonomy and the relevance of vision and mission to strategy have been considered in Chapters 2 and 3 and you may now wish to refer back to these chapters before moving on to a more detailed analysis of the planning process and its implementation.

At this stage, it may be useful to clarify the relationship between:

- strategic thinking and management;
- strategic planning; and
- development planning.

Although the terms strategic management and strategic planning may be used interchangeably at times, strategic management is 'much more than strategic planning' (Middlewood, 1998, p. 10). Strategic planning relates to the implementation of the vision that is implicit in strategic management. In the following quotation, intentions relate to the vision of management and strategies to the more practical application of strategic planning: 'good intentions don't move mountains; bulldozers do. In non-profit management, the mission and the plan... are the good intentions. Strategies are the bulldozers' (Drucker, 1990, p. 45).

In reviewing strategic management in schools and colleges, Middlewood and Lumby (1998, p. x) state that: 'Strategic management involves taking a view of the whole organization, its key purpose, its direction and its place in its environment.' West-Burnham, (1994b, p. 82) likens strategic planning in an educational institution to 'a matter of bridge building or mapping the route between the perceived present situation and the desired future situation'.

The term strategic planning generally covers an extended timescale of three to five years. In schools, the term development planning usually relates to a shorter timescale of about a year. In colleges where the emphasis is very much on strategic planning, the overall plan is likely to be known as the corporate or strategic plan and from that would be developed shorter-term plans referred to as business plans or action plans (Lumby, 1998, p. 92). These shorter-term plans for about a year, whether called development plans or business plans, typically include targets and performance indicators and indicate details of specific action.

Although a key note of strategic planning is its long-term nature, Weindling (1997) provides several distinctions between long-term planning and strategic planning. Perhaps the most telling of these distinctions is the closed, rational nature of long-term planning and the open and dynamic nature of strategic planning.

Who is involved in strategic planning?

There is an implicit hierarchy in consideration of longer-term strategic planning and shorter-term development planning and implementation. For example, in schools, strategy may be seen as the province of senior management, development planning as involving middle management and operational activities classroom teachers. West-Burnham (1994b) argues that this need not be the case:

1. In schools, individuals may work at all three levels.
2. The process is dynamic, depending upon interaction between levels.
3. A hierarchy of functions does not necessarily require a hierarchy in status.
4. The project or taskforce may be an ideal way to solve problems and generate policies.

Earley (1998, p. 150) also argues for the involvement of all staff:

> It has become increasingly apparent that for organisations to survive in an increasingly turbulent and changing environment, issues of strategy can no longer simply be seen as the exclusive preserve of senior staff. For strategy to be successfully implemented, staff at all levels in an organisation increasingly need to be involved in decision-making and policy formulation – albeit to varying degrees – and be encouraged to develop a sense of ownership and share the organisation's mission.

However, the involvement of staff in strategic management, particularly in larger organisations like further education colleges, will be problematic: 'Given the perceptions that consultation is too slow, that staff may be too busy, uninterested, sceptical of the whole process and determined to resist change, it is not surprising that some principals and senior management teams may argue against the involvement of a large number of staff' (Lumby, 1998, p. 97).

On the whole, it seems clear that the responsibility for strategy is firmly located with senior management, but that the involvement and understanding of all is desirable. Caldwell and Spinks (1992, pp. 91–2) argue that:

> Strategic leadership is distinguished from ongoing, routine, day-to-day leadership on three dimensions: time, scale of issue and scope of action...

> Leaders other than principals will exercise strategic leadership in a self-managing school, especially leaders of programmes teams. The scale of action may have a focus on individual programmes but school-wide considerations are paramount.

The issues in colleges may be complicated by scale and the resulting possibility of more disparate and even countervailing views:

> One difficulty in using the strategic planning process...is a scepticism in the minds of many staff that the plan really is a serious statement of the purpose of the corporation, and particularly of the chief executive's real intentions and priorities. I do all I can...so that staff feel that their contributions to the plan and their familiarity with it really does get to the heart of what is in the mind of the principal, the chair of the corporation, and other key decision-makers (Bridge, 1994, p. 192).

Limb (1992, p. 172) describes a model of a planning process that does ensure the involvement of middle managers at two stages, the formulation of college-wide priorities and the agreement of the specific components of the strategy relevant to each curriculum area by the staff in that area:

> It is the task of the Director and the three Assistant Directors to consider the individual plans of each middle manager in order to synthesize their key points. In this way the directorate devised a yearly annual programme and a rolling three-year development plan for the college. The Director and governors gave an indication of the overall pace of change in the light of available resources and whole college organizational capabilities.

Whilst the locus of power may rest with the senior management, particularly the headteacher or principal, the need for involvement and consultation is generally recognised, particularly in schools. This is likely to be more difficult in colleges given the large numbers of staff who might potentially be involved.

However, the potential impact of external pressures, particularly of statutory change, cannot be ignored. Schools and colleges are both subject to such pressures. Primary schools in England and Wales have had to incorporate into their development plans the demands of the 'Literacy Hour'. Similarly schools in South Africa are having to adopt 'Outcomes-Based Education', a new style of teaching and assessment. It could be argued that, for colleges of further education in England and Wales, the context of the planning process, dictated by external imperatives, considerably limits the freedom of action in determining the nature and priorities of the strategic plan.

◉ Reading and **Activity**

List five factors which might inhibit strategic planning within your organisation. Note whether their origin is internal or external to your school or college.

You may like to read 'Strategic Planning in Further Education' by Jacky Lumby, Chapter 7 in Middlewood, D. and Lumby, J. (eds.) *Strategic Management in Schools and Colleges*, with special reference to pp. 91–4, for an indication of the numbers and types of external constraints that might impinge on the strategic planning process in a further education college.

❏ Comment

There is likely to be a range of factors that are individual to each institution but, in addition to the constraints imposed by national government, factors such as the competitiveness of neighbouring institutions may be of over-riding importance in identifying strategic aims.

In the chapter recommended above, Lumby points out the range of factors that limit the freedom of colleges to define their own priorities. These include the imposition of financial regimes which include the tensions resulting from continuing demands for efficiency gains and also relate to the ambiguous position of colleges in operating partially within the public sector and partially within a competitive business environment.

Development planning

Although the term development planning is usually applied to the annual planning process in schools in the UK, the process that is involved in development planning has a degree of applicability to any planning cycle in any educational institution.

Development planning may be defined as a short-term process (one year) identifying how the strategic plan is to be implemented. The following definition of development planning emphasises the importance placed on the *process* of planning:

> Development *planning* is more than a development *plan*, the document: it is the process of creating the plan and then ensuring that it is put into effect. The plan is a statement of intentions which reflect the school's vision for the future. The process involves reaching agreement on a sensible set of priorities for the school and then taking action to realise the plan (Hargreaves and Hopkins, 1991, p. 3, emphasis in original).

In England and Wales, the Education Reform Act made development planning a statutory duty for schools, and the School Development Plans project led by Hargreaves was funded by the DES from April

1989 to August 1990. As a result two booklets on the nature and process of development planning were circulated to schools, and many LEAs followed this with their own advice to their schools. Even where planning is not statutory, schools and colleges are likely to find there are advantages in adopting a regular planning cycle.

❏ The process of planning

Whatever the scale of a plan and whatever the size of the institution, the planning process requires the posing of four questions:

1. Where are we?
2. What changes do we need to make?
3. How shall we manage these changes over time?
4. How shall we know whether our management of change has been successful?

Hargreaves and Hopkins (1991, p. 4) identify the equivalent four main processes, specifically for development planning in schools, but which apply to every planning process:

- *Audit*: a school reviews its strengths and weaknesses.
- *Construction*: priorities for development are selected and then turned into specific targets.
- *Implementation*: the planned priorities and targets are implemented.
- *Evaluation*: the success of implementation is checked.

The remainder of this section will consider the four stages of audit, construction, implementation and evaluation.

An *audit* will reveal both strengths and weaknesses of the institution at the time. It will thus enable decisions to be made concerning priorities for action and will require examination of the match between the resources that are available and intended provision.

Skelton *et al.* (1991) offer these principles for carrying out the audit:

1. Keep in mind the purpose of the audit.
2. Strike a balance between self justification and self-flagellation.
3. Emphasis the strengths as well as the weaknesses.
4. Make sure that all of these six areas are covered:
    - the whole curriculum
    - the whole staff
    - the school constituency
    - buildings and sites
    - organisational systems
    - the climate or atmosphere within
5. Appreciate the need to involve others.
6. Take into account the professional and personal lives of those concerned (adapted from *ibid.*, 1991).

The audit should take into account any recent reviews of the school, the targets that have been set at appraisal interviews and the views of all stakeholder groups, including parents, students, staff, governors and the wider community.

The question as to who carries out the audit is answered by Hargreaves and Hopkins (1991) by the recommendation that the areas for specific audit are selected by the headteacher following discussions with governors and staff and that the actual responsibility for carrying out the audit is handled by one teacher or a team of teachers.

The construction and implementation of the plan will be set within the context of the aims and values of the school, but are likely to be based on a system of consultation informed by the audit process. The consultation will lead to the establishment of priorities. Hargreaves and Hopkins (*ibid.*) state that the choice of priorities for the construction of the plan should be guided by two principles. The plan (*ibid.*, p. 42) must be:

manageable: the risk of trying to do too much too quickly must be avoided;

coherent: the priorities must be placed in a sequence that makes implementation easier.

❏ An example of the phases of development planning in a middle school

The senior management of Bridgewater Middle School in Hertfordshire decided to revisit the area of development planning. The new deputy head undertook an audit in the form of a SWOT analysis with students, parents, lunchtime supervisors and governors. Consultation also took place with their LEA inspector. A training day for all staff took place out of school. The day incorporated a presentation of the views collected in the audit process, but was primarily to allow a consultation process with staff to take place. From this day emerged the following priority areas for incorporation into the development plan:

1. The overall importance of pupil attitude and motivation and the need to have high expectations.
2. Home–school communication.
3. The issue of time-tabling relating both to the deployment of staff and the use of space within the school.
4. Monitoring and evaluating the quality of teaching.
5. Increasing the use of IT across the curriculum.
6. The need for detailed termly/yearly departmental plans for the curriculum.

These priorities were honed by the senior management team and governors to become the following main points for the development plan:

Bridgewater School Development Plan 1997 – 2001

To raise levels of achievement:

- to create a timetable that implements the curriculum most effectively
- to improve the quality of teaching/learning
- to raise levels of motivation and expectations

To improve levels of communication

To improve the facilities at Bridgewater

To increase the use of IT across the curriculum

Each of these areas was further subdivided. For example, the raising of levels of motivation and expectations (a subset of the major priority, 'to raise levels of achievement') was considered in terms of not only pupils but staff and others. Thus, in terms of the expectations of others, one of the actions included in the plan was to 're-examine the projected image of the school.' In each case, responsibilities were allotted to individuals, along with timescales for implementation and evaluation and an indication of the costs implied.

At the same time, the aims of the school were revisited, and the priorities for planning can be seen to relate to these aims:

1. To create and maintain a caring and secure setting where pupils can achieve their full potential.
2. To enable pupils to experience success, build self-esteem and be happy, leading to a positive view for their future life and encourage life-long learning.
3. To enable every pupil to become an active participant in individual achievement.
4. To promote moral values and respect for different religious and cultural beliefs.
5. To foster co-operation between pupils, parents, teachers, governors, businesses and friends of the school.
6. To be accountable to parents for progress and standards.
7. To promote opportunities for the development of staff.

Consultation continues with stakeholders, particularly governors and staff who are involved in active review and prioritisation on an annual basis (Bridgewater Middle School Development Plan, 1997–98).

❏ Action plans

Hargreaves and Hopkins (1991, p. 5) recommend that, for each year of the development plan, each of the priorities of the plan should be turned into a set of detailed action plans, where an action plan is 'a working document which describes and summarises what needs to be done to implement and evaluate a priority. It serves as a guide to implementation and helps to monitor progress and success.'

If each priority is turned into a set of targets each target can then be divided into a set of tasks for which one person is responsible. The achievement of targets can be measured by success criteria which 'are a means for evaluating the outcomes of the plan, as well as providing benchmarks for development' (*ibid.*, p. 51).

The fourth stage of the planning process is *evaluation*. It is important that evaluation of the progress of the plan takes place as part of the cycle. The intention is that what has been achieved will be measured against stated aims before the school or college moves on to the next step. With strategic planning, this may be problematic as the extended time-frame makes detailed monitoring difficult. To some extent problems may be overcome by viewing strategic planning not as a series, but as a continuous process 'of more or less continual creation, monitoring and adjustment of the rolling plans' (Wallace, 1991, p. 190).

Evaluation and monitoring are not synonymous (Hardie, 1998), monitoring taking place throughout the process, and evaluation takes place at the end of a specific period, usually a year.

Hargreaves and Hopkins (1991) refer to evaluation by teachers using their professional judgement and backing this up by the collection of complementary evidence. By complementary evidence, they mean a range of sources providing both quantitative and qualitative data which might include the following:

- Observation, both of pupils and around the school.
- Obtaining the views and opinions of those concerned in the changes brought about by the planning process. They particularly mention the importance of obtaining the views of students.
- Written materials, such as teachers' records and pupils' work.
- Statistical information, such as trends in attendance rates.
- More formal research, perhaps undertaken by teachers undertaking postgraduate training, such as an MBA in educational management.

In all cases, it is stressed that the collection of data for the evaluation process should be undertaken in a systematic manner, and should not rely on anecdotal evidence.

◎ Reading and **Activity**

What methods of evaluation are used in your school or college to evaluate aspects of the development or business plan? Which personnel are involved in the evaluation process?

You may now wish to read 'Managing monitoring and evaluation' by Brian Hardie, Chapter 12 in Middlewood, D. and Lumby, J. (eds) *Strategic Management in Schools and Colleges*, which presents an overview of the relationship of evaluation to strategy, particularly considering how evaluation can be related to strategy and to the interests of stakeholders.

❏ Comment

It may be that evaluation is not carried out systematically in your school or college, or that the responsibility is not clearly delineated. Alternatively it may be that the evaluation takes place, but that the outcome is not built into the ongoing planning process. MacGilchrist *et al.* (1997, p. 213) found, in their research in primary schools, that evaluation was the weakest element of the planning process, although in some schools where better practice was observed: 'The headteachers and the class teachers in the schools were demonstrating the characteristics of reflective practitioners. They were constantly evaluating progress and seeking to improve the process.'

Hardie (1998) considers that the evaluation of stakeholder expectations is critical. He also identifies levels of evaluation, strategic, tactical and operational, which would seem to imply the equivalent evaluation on the part of the senior management, the middle management and also at the classroom level. The participation in evaluation of those affected by the planning process is also stressed. The idea of involvement and ownership is further considered in the next section on management of the planning process.

Management style and development planning

The role of management in the planning process is seen by Hargreaves and Hopkins (1991) as being the *empowerment* of all concerned in the process. However, in such a scenario senior managers are responsible for ensuring that the arrangements necessary to support development planning are in place. These arrangements are identified by Hargreaves and Hopkins (*ibid.*) as ensuring:

1. frameworks, such as having written policy statements, the establishment of short-term task groups and setting up procedures for evaluation and checks on quality of progress;
2. clarification of roles and responsibilities for governors, heads and staff;
3. promotion of collaboration and co-ordination both within the school and between the school and its partners (adapted from *ibid.*, p. 16).

Above all, the role of the management may be to ensure the involvement of the stakeholders in the planning process: 'If the staff are not to perceive school development plans as imposed documents, threatening accountability, they need to be involved in the planning and decision-making process' (Davies and Ellison, 1992, p. 71).

Research undertaken by Cuckle *et al.* (1998) would seem to indicate that progress has been made in the involvement of teaching staff, if not others, in development planning. A large-scale survey and interviews with primary schools produced the following findings:

there was widespread involvement of teaching staff (but not teaching support staff, parents, children or governors) in development planning;

staff generally found SDPs to be beneficial;

governors' knowledge and involvement varied considerably both *within* and *between* schools;

headteachers had overall responsibility for SDPs – this was generally approved and staff take part in development planning within the context of their school (adapted from *ibid.*, p. 194).

However, the research project led by MacGilchrist and Mortimore (1997) identified a typology of plans, including the following:

- The rhetorical plan – where there is a lack of a shared sense of ownership and purpose.
- The singular plan – owned by only the headteacher.
- The co-operative plan – characterised by the co-operative effort to improve with partial ownership of the staff.
- The corporate plan – characterised by a corporate effort to improve with evidence of a learning community.

The co-operative and corporate plans appeared to be more effective in a number of ways. In these schools:

- Classroom observation over two years showed that the pupils worked harder, co-operated well with each other and were more self-disciplined.
- Classroom observation also showed that the teachers gave the pupils more responsibility and gave the pupils more praise; they were also regarded as more interesting and better organised.
- The development planning process was being used to identify priorities for development.
- There was a growing sophistication in the strategies used to implement the plan.
- Although remaining a relative weakness, there was better practice in terms of evaluation.

One area of weakness that was identified across all schools was the lack of the identification of success criteria at the stage of the formulation of the plan (based on MacGilchrist and Mortimore, *ibid.*)

The difficulties of involving staff in further education colleges in the planning process have already been referred to. Lumby (1998), recognising the difficulties of involving large numbers of staff, refers to the order in which the planning is done. Is the strategic plan an amalgam of development plans from subunits, or are the subunits plans developed in the light of the circulated strategic plan? In addition:

> There is a tension between the need to create ownership by allowing sub-units of the college to contribute their own strategic aims to a central plan, and the need for a whole-college approach, which would have to be mediated by one group, often senior management, at the risk of appearing remote and irrelevant to the mass of staff in the college (*ibid.*, p. 97).

 Reading

Now please read 'Effective school development planning' by Edith Jayne, Chapter 6 of Middlewood, D. and Lumby, J. (eds.) *Strategic Management in Schools and Colleges*. This chapter reviews the history, purposes and processes involved in development planning and provides two case studies.

❑ Comment
Both schools in the case study show how development planning can be used in the process of the management of change. The management of change will be considered further in the following brief section, and in more detail in Chapter 8.

Development planning, improvement and effectiveness and change

The origins of school development planning lie in the move towards school improvement and effectiveness. The recognition that schools can differentially affect their pupils gives strength and purpose to school improvement and development planning: 'the research suggests that teachers and schools have more control than they may have imagined over their ability to change their present direction and become efficient and effective agents of pupils' learning and development' (Hopkins, 1987 p. 3).

Development planning is linked with school improvement and is a means of managing change. Hopkins (1994a) sees development planning as helping a school to organise what it is doing in a purposeful and coherent way and also helping them to manage innovation and change. However, it is not suggested that development planning alone can act to bring about successful change: 'successful change efforts have come about without the formulation of a plan, and…having a plan is no guarantee of successfully managing educational change' (Hutchinson, 1993, p. 7).

Much that is written about strategic planning is based on the assumption that there is a clear sequential logic, each element being contingent on the one preceding it, and there may be an implicit assumption that the outcomes are unproblematic. In effect, planning may be seen as a panacea. The expectations of rational planning may not always sit comfortably with the reality of educational organisations where educational policy-making may impinge on plans (Lumby, 1998) and where those who are involved in planning may not always have the necessary skills and knowledge. In addition, planning may be subject to micro-political processes. Marsh D. (1992, p. 114) identifies a process of planning where 'alternatives are often formulated and defended before the issue has been clearly stated. Feelings run high. Personal preferences are expressed in the same breath with reasoned arguments'.

It would certainly appear that planning is likely to be most successful where there is a shared culture and understanding within a school or college. FEU (undated) describes how one college of further education developed a strategy through a process of involvement and consultation:

> they found that the consultative process had enabled staff to reflect upon their own work and on its significance to the development of the whole institution. It had ensured 'staff ownership' of the college aims and a sharing of values and goals. It was particularly noticeable that listening, dialogue and feedback was important to all staff (quoted in West-Burnham *et al.*, 1995, p. 60).

This largely coincides with Wallace's (1991, p. 133) summary of Louis and Miles' (1990) view of evolutionary planning which argues that the effective response is to 'cycle back and forth between efforts to gain normative consensus about what it may become, to plan strategies for getting there, and to carry out decentralised, incremental experimentation that harnesses the creativity of all members to the change effort'.

It is the processes of 'normative consensus' and 'incremental experimentation' that may best support the process of rational planning to bring about change and improvement.

❏ **Building on key learning points**

- Strategic and development planning are essential aspects of management of schools and colleges and may be differentiated by scale.
- Involvement of stakeholders appears to make the planning processes more successful, but in larger organisations, such as colleges, such involvement is logistically difficult to achieve.
- Planning is key to the processes of change and improvement.

---

8. Managing strategic change

Throughout this book we have been at pains to emphasise that change is at the heart of management and leadership. We have noted the increase in the pace of legislative change in many countries as governments seek to harness education to a drive for economic growth. In some, but not all, cases these changes are linked to the introduction of self-management for educational organisations. In most countries, there has been a drive for accountability linked to inspection and/or other forms of external evaluation.

Change may also arise from internally generated innovation, linked to the strategic perspective discussed in this book. Developing vision and mission seems bound to lead to the introduction of new ideas except in those rare cases where the review concludes with a 'steady as you go' prescription. The switch to self-management locates more levers of control at school level and provides the potential for internally generated change. Whether it is externally or internally stimulated, change is inevitable and the plaintive cries for 'a period of stability', emanating from institutions and their professional organisations, seem forlorn. No change is not an option. Lumby (1998, p. 191) states that 'change arises from multiple sources... all in the context of the need to survive in an increasingly competitive environment'.

Change may be externally imposed or derive from internal review but, in either case, it requires effective management. Leaders need to establish the climate, the structures and the processes to enable new ideas to be forged, tested and implemented for the benefit of pupils and students. They also need to be able to adjudicate between competing priorities and to determine whether and how to resource new initiatives.

Strategic change may be characterised by its extended timescale and its wide scope, as we noted earlier (p. 3). Internally generated change ought also to be consistent with the priorities identified through strategic planning although such rational assumptions are not always fulfilled in complex organisations such as schools, colleges and universities. It may also match external imperatives if leaders have been able to anticipate national and international trends through 'scenario planning'.

◎ Reading and **Activity**

Please now read Jacky Lumby's 'Understanding strategic change', Chapter 14 in Middlewood, D. and Lumby, J. (eds.) *Strategic Management in Schools and Colleges*.

As you read, consider her main points and consider which may apply in your organisation.

❑ Comment

Lumby raises many important issues in this chapter but the most significant may be the following:

- Change is unavoidable; 'an ever-present reality'.
- The experience of change is 'often bleak'.
- Defining success criteria for change is 'elusive'.
- Successful change in education takes time; 'no quick fix'.
- Change is likely to be resisted by internal and external networks through what are essentially political processes.

- Collegial processes are desirable to promote 'ownership' but these may be supplanted by political mechanisms.
- Given the difficulties of implementation, 'partial success is a matter of pride'.

It is obviously not possible for the authors to speculate about your experience of change but it is probable that you will have encountered at least some of the phenomena identified by Lumby. Certainly, the notion of interest groups resisting change, particularly in larger organisations, is likely to be familiar to many educators.

Despite the problematic nature of both strategic management and change, reinforcing the ambiguity model discussed earlier, the search for a strategic perspective is essential. The alternative of a purely reactive stance, responding to events as they arise, is always likely to leave the organisation behind its rivals. In an increasingly competitive and turbulent environment, that would be a recipe for stagnation and possible decline. Change may be uncomfortable, and strategic management may be difficult and uncertain, but one is inevitable and the other provides the best prospect of an appropriate response.

References

Baldridge, J., Curtis, D., Ecker, G. and Riley, G. (1978) *Policy Making and Effective Leadership*, San Francisco, CA, Jossey-Bass.

Bass, B.M. (1981) *Stogdill's Handbook of Leadership: A Survey of Theory and Research*, Glencoe, IL, Free Press.

Bass, B.M. and Avolio, B.J. (1994) *Improving Organizational Effectiveness through Transformational Leadership*, Thousand Oaks, CA, Sage.

Beare, H., Caldwell, B. and Millikan, R. (1989a) *Creating an Excellent School*, London, Routledge.

Beare, H., Caldwell, B.J. and Millikan, R.H. (1989b) *Creating an Excellent School: Some New Management Techniques*, London, Routledge.

Beare, H., Caldwell, B. and Millikan, R. (1993) 'Leadership', in Preedy, M. (ed.) *Managing the Effective School*, London, Paul Chapman Publishing.

Belbin, R.M. (1981) *Management Teams: Why they Succeed or Fail*, Oxford, Heinemann Professional.

Bem, S.L. (1974) 'The measurement of psychological androgyny', *Journal of Consulting and Clinical Psychology*, Vol. 42, no. 2, pp. 155–62.

Bennis, W. (1984) 'Transformative power and leadership', in Sergiovanni, T. and Corbally, J. (eds.) *Leadership and Organizational Culture*, Urbana, IL, and Chicago, IL, University of Illinois Press.

Bennis, W. and Nanus, B. (1985) *Leaders*, New York, Harper & Row.

Bjerke, B. and Al-Meer, A. (1993) 'Culture's consequences: management in Saudi Arabia', in *Leadership and Organization Development Journal*, Vol. 14, no. 2. pp. 30–5.

Blackmore, J. (1989) 'Educational leadership: a feminist critique and reconstruction' in Smyth, I. and John, W. (eds.) *Critical Perspectives on Educational Leadership, Deakin Studies In Education Series ?*, Lewes, Falmer Press.

Blake, R.R. and Mouton, J.S. (1964) *The Managerial Grid*, Houston, TX, Gulf Publishing.

Block, P. (1987) *The Empowered Manager*, San Francisco, CA, Jossey-Bass.

Blum, R. and Butler, J. (1989) 'The role of school leaders in school improvement', in Blum, R. and Butler, J. (eds.), *School Leader Development for School Improvement*, Leuven, Acco.

Bolam, R., McMahon, A., Pocklington, K. and Weindling, D. (1993) *Effective Management in Schools*, London, HMSO.

Bolman, L. and Deal, T. (1984) *Modern Approaches to Understanding and Managing Organisations*, San Francisco, CA, Jossey-Bass.

Bolman, L. and Deal, T. (1991) *Reforming Organisations: Artistry, Choice and Leadership*, San Francisco, CA, Jossey-Bass.

Bottery, M. (1992) *The Ethics of Educational Management*, London, Cassell.

Bowring-Carr, C. and West-Burnham, J. (1997) *Effective Learning in Schools*, London, Pitman Publishing

Bridge, W. (1994) 'Change where contrasting cultures meet', in Gorringe, R. and Toogood, P. (eds.), *Changing the Culture of a College, Coombe Lodge Report, 24, 3*, Bristol, Further Education Staff College.

Bryant, M.T., (1998) 'Cross-cultural understandings of leadership: themes from Native American interviews', *Educational Management and Administration*, Vol. 26, no. 1, pp. 7–20.

Bullock, A. and Thomas, H. (1997) *Schools at the Centre?*, London, Routledge.

Burnham, P. (1969) 'Role theory and educational administration', in Baron, G. and Taylor, W. (eds.) *Educational Administration and the Social Sciences*, London, The Athlone Press.

Burns, J.M. (1978) *Leadership*, New York, Harper & Row.

Bush, T. (1994) 'Theory and practice in educational management', in Bush, T. and West-Burnham, J. (eds.) *The Principles of Educational Management*, Harlow, Longman.

Bush, T. (1995) *Theories of Educational Management* (second edition), London, Paul Chapman Publishing.

Bush, T. (1997) 'The changing context of management in education', in Bush, T. and Middlewood, D. (eds.) *Managing People in Education*, London, Paul Chapman Publishing.

Bush, T. (1998) 'Organisational culture and strategic management', in Middlewood, D. and Lumby, J. (eds.) *Strategic Management in Schools and Colleges*, London, Paul Chapman Publishing.

Bush, T., Coleman, M. and Glover, D. (1993) *Managing Autonomous Schools: The Grant-Maintained Experience*, London, Paul Chapman Publishing.

Bush T. and West-Burnham, J. (eds.) (1994) *The Principles of Educational Management*, Harlow, Longman.

Caldwell, B. and Spinks, J. (1988) *The Self-Managing School*, London, Falmer Press.

Caldwell, B. and Spinks, J. (1992) *Leading the Self-Managing School*, London, Falmer Press.

Capper, C.A. and Jamison, M.T. (1993) 'Let the buyer beware: total quality management and educational research and practice', *Educational Researcher*, Vol. 22, no. 8, pp. 15–30.

Carlson, R. (1975) 'Environmental constraints and organizational consequences: the public school and its clients', in Baldridge, J. and Deal, T. (eds.) *Managing Change in Educational Organizations*, Berkeley, CA, McCutchan.

CERI (1995) *Schools under Scrutiny: Strategies for the Evaluation of School Performance*, Paris, OECD.

Chapman, J. (1993) 'Leadership, school-based decision making and school effectiveness', in Dimmock, C. (ed.) *School Based Management and School Effectiveness*, London, Routledge.

Chow, W.S. and Luk, W. (1996) 'Management in the 1990s: A comparative study of women managers', *Journal of Managerial Psychology*, Vol. 11, no. 1, pp. 24–36.

Coleman, M. (1994a) 'Leadership in educational management', in Bush, T. and West-Burnham, J. (eds.) *The Principles of Educational Management*, Harlow, Longman.

Coleman, M. (1994b) 'Women in educational management', in Bush, T. and West-Burnham, J. (eds.) *The Principles of Educational Management*, Harlow, Longman.

Coleman, M. (1996) 'Barriers to career progress for women in education: the perceptions of female headteachers', *Educational Research*, Vol. 38, no. 3, pp. 317–332.

Coleman, M. (1996) 'Management style of female headteachers', *Educational Management and Administration*, Vol. 24, no. 2, pp. 163–174.

Coleman, M. (2000) 'The female secondary headteacher in England and Wales: leadership and management styles', *Educational Research*, Vol. 42, no. 1, pp. 13–27.

Coleman, M., Qiang, H. and Li, Y. (1998) 'Women in educational management in China: experience in Shaanxi Province', *Compare*, Vol. 28. no. 2, pp. 141–54.

Collins, C. and Porras, J. (1991) 'Organisational vision and visionary organisations', *California Management Review*, Fall, pp. 30–52.

Coopers & Lybrand (1988) *Local Management of Schools: A Report to the DES*, London, HMSO.

Cotton, K. (1994) *Applying Total Quality Management Principles to Secondary Education: Mt Edgecumbe High School, Sitka, Alaska. School Improvement Research Series*, Portland, OR, Northwest Regional Educational Laboratory.

Coulson, A. (1974) 'The deputy head in the primary school: role conceptions of heads and deputy heads', unpublished MEd thesis, University of Hull.

Creemers, B.P.M. and Reezigt, G.R. (1997) 'School effectiveness and school improvement: sustaining links', in *School Effectiveness and School Improvement*, Vol. 8, no. 4, pp. 396–429.

Cuckle, P., Broadhead, P., Hodgson, J. and Dunford, J. (1998) 'Development planning in primary schools: a positive influence on management and culture', *Educational Management and Administration*, Vol. 26, no. 2, pp. 185–195.

Culbertson, J. (1983) 'Theory in educational administration: echoes from critical thinkers', *Educational Researcher*, Vol. 12, no. 10, pp. 15–22.

Cuthbert, R. (1984) 'The management process', in *E324 Management in Post Compulsory Education, Block 3, Part 2*, Milton Keynes, Open University Press.

Cyert, R. (1975) *The Management of Non-Profit Organizations*, Lexington, MA, Lexington Books.

Davies, B. (1994) 'Models of decision-making in resource allocation' in Bush, T. and West-Burnham, J. (eds.) *The Principles of Educational Management*, Harlow, Longman.

Davies, B. and Ellison, L. (1992) *School Development Planning*, Harlow, Longman.

Davies, B. and West-Burnham, J. (1997) *Reengineering and Total Quality in Schools*, London, Pitman Publishing.

Davies, L. (1997) 'The rise of the school effectiveness movement', in White, J. and Barber, M. (eds.) *Perspectives on School Effectiveness and School Improvement*, London, University of London, Institute of

Education.

Davies, L. and Gunawardena, C. (1992) *Women and Men in Educational Management: An International Inquiry, IIEP Research Report No. 95*, Paris, International Institute for Educational Planning.

Deal, T. (1988) 'The symbolism of effective schools', in Westoby, A. (ed.) *Culture and Power in Educational Organisations*, Milton Keynes, Open University Press.

Dimmock, C. (1998) 'Restructuring Hong Kong's schools: the applicability of western theories, policies and practices to an Asian culture', *Educational Management and Administration*, Vol. 26, no. 4, pp. 363–77.

Drucker, P.F. (1990) *Managing the Non-Profit Organization*, London, Butterworth-Heinemann.

Duignan, P.A. and Macpherson, R.J.S. (1992) 'Educative leadership for quality teaching: a synthesis and a commentary', in Duignan, P.A. and Macpherson, R.J.S. (eds.) *Educative Leadership: A Practical Theory for New Administrators and Managers*, London, Falmer Press.

Earley, P. (1998) 'Middle management – the key to organisational success?', in Middlewood, D. and Lumby, J. (eds.) *Strategic Management in Schools and Colleges*, London, Paul Chapman Publishing.

Education Department, Hong Kong (1993) *Aided Schools General Circular No 12/93: The School Management Initiative (SMI)*, Hong Kong, Education Department.

Education Department, Hong Kong (1998) *Quality Assurance Inspection Annual Report, 1997/98*, Hong Kong, Education Department.

Everard, K. and Morris, G. (1990) *Effective School Management*, London, Paul Chapman Publishing.

Evers, C. and Lakomski, G. (1991) 'Educational administration as a science: a post-positivist proposal', in Ribbins, P., Glatter, R., Simkins, T. and Watson, L. (eds.) *Developing Educational Leaders*, Harlow, Longman.

FEFC (1993) *Assessing Achievement*, Coventry, FEFC.

FEFC (1997) *Quality and Standards in Further Education in England, 1996–97*, Coventry, FEFC.

FEFC (1998) *Performance Indicators 1996–97*, London, HMSO.

Ferrario, M. (1994) 'Women as managerial leaders', in Davidson, M.J. and Burke, R.J. (eds.) *Women in Management: Current Research Issues*, London, Paul Chapman.

FEU (1995) *Making Quality your Own: A Discussion Paper*, Bristol, FEU.

FEU (undated) *Challenges for Colleges*, London, FEU.

Fidler, B. (1997) 'School leadership: some key ideas', *School Leadership and Management*, Vol. 17, no. 1, pp. 23–37.

Foreman, K. (1998) 'Vision and mission', in Middlewood, D. and Lumby, J. (eds.) *Strategic Management in Schools in Colleges*, London, Paul Chapman Publishing.

Foskett, N. (1998) 'Linking marketing to strategy', in Middlewood, D. and Lumby, J. (eds.) *Strategic Management in Schools and Colleges*, London, Paul Chapman Publishing.

Fullan, M. (1991) *The New Meaning of Educational Change*, London, Cassell.

Fullan, M. (1992), 'Causes/processes of implementation and continuation', in Bennett, N., Crawford, M. and Riches, C. (eds.) *Managing Change in Education*, London, Paul Chapman Publishing.

Gane, V. and Morgan, A. (1992) *Managing Headteacher Appraisal*, London, Paul Chapman Publishing.

Gaziel, H. (1998) 'School-based management as a factor in school effectiveness', *International Review of Educating*, Vol. 44, no. 4, pp. 319–33.

Glatter, R. (1979) 'Educational policy and management: one field or two', *Educational Analysis*, Vol. 1, no. 2, pp. 15–24.

Glatter, R. (1997) 'Context and capability in educational management', *Educational Management and Administration*, Vol. 25, no. 2, pp. 181–92.

Glatter, R. and Weindling, D. (1993), 'Strategies for development', in *E326 Managing Schools: Challenge and Response*, Milton Keynes, The Open University.

Glover, D., Levačić R., Bennett, N. and Earley, P. (1996) 'Leadership planning and resource management in four very effective schools: part I setting the scene', *School Organisation*, Vol. 16. no. 2, pp. 135–148.

Goldring, E. and Chen, M. (1994) 'The feminization of the principalship in Israel: the trade-off between political power and co-operative leadership', in Marshall, C. (ed.) *The New Politics of Race and Gender*, London, Falmer Press.

Goldring, E. and Pasternak, R. (1994) 'Principals' co-ordinating strategies and school effectiveness',

Schools Effectiveness and School Improvement, Vol. 5, no, 3, pp. 239–53.

Grace, G. (1995) *School Leadership*, London, Falmer Press.

Gray, H. (1979) 'Personal viewpoint: organisations as subjectivities', *Educational Administration*, Vol. 7, no. 2, pp. 122–9.

Gray, H.L. (1989) 'Gender considerations in school management: masculine and feminine leadership styles', in Riches, C. and Morgan, C. (eds.) *Human Resource Management in Education*, Milton Keynes, Open University Press.

Gray, H.L. (1993) 'Gender issues in management training', in Ozga, J. (ed.) *Women in Educational Management*, Buckingham, Open University Press.

Gray, J. (1995) 'The quality of schooling: frameworks for judgement', in Gray, J. and Wilcox, B. (eds.) *Good School, Bad School: Evaluating Performance and Encouraging Improvement*, Buckingham, Open University Press.

Gray, J. (1998) 'The contribution of educational research to the cause of school improvement', lecture, London, Institute of Education.

Hackett, G. (1998) 'League tables just on target for 2002', *The Times Educational Supplement, School and College Performance Tables 1998*, December.

Hall, V. (1996) *Dancing on the Ceiling: A Study of Women Managers in Education*, London, Paul Chapman Publishing.

Hall, V. (1997) 'Management roles in education', in Bush, T. and Middlewood, D. (eds.) *Managing People in Education, London*, Paul Chapman Publishing.

Hall, V. (1998) 'Strategic leadership in education: becoming, being, doing', in Middlewood, D. and Lumby, J. (eds.) *Strategic Management in Schools and Colleges*, London, Paul Chapman Publishing.

Hall, V., Mackay, H. and Morgan, D. (1986) *Headteachers at Work*, Milton Keynes, Open University Press.

Hammer, M. and Champy, J. (1993) *Reengineering the Corporation: A Manifesto for Business Revolution*, London, Nicholas Brealey Publishing.

Harber, C. and Davies, L. (1997) *School Management and Effectiveness in Developing Countries: The Post-Bureaucratic School*, London, Cassell.

Harbison, R. and Hanushek, E. (1992) *Educational Performance of the Poor: Lessons from North-East Brazil*, Washington, DC, World Bank.

Hardie, B. (1998) 'Managing monitoring and evaluation', in Middlewood, D. and Lumby, J. (eds.) *Strategic Management in Schools and Colleges*, London, Paul Chapman Publishing.

Hargreaves, D. (1994) *The Mosaic of Learning: Schools and Teachers for the New Century*, London, Demos.

Hargreaves, D. (1997) 'School culture, school effectiveness and school improvement', in Harris, A., Bennett, N. and Preedy, M. (eds.) *Organizational Effectiveness and Improvement in Education*, Buckingham, Open University Press.

Hargreaves, D. and Hopkins, D. (1991) *The Empowered School*, London, Cassell.

Harris, A. (1998) 'Improving ineffective departments in secondary schools: strategies for change and development', *Educational Management and Administration*, Vol. 26, no. 3, pp. 269–78.

Higher Education Quality Council (HEQC) (1996) *Guidelines on Quality Assurance, 1996.* London, HEQC.

Hodgkinson, C. (1991) *Educational Leadership: The Moral Art*, Albany, NY, State University of New York Press.

Hofstede, G. (1980) *Culture's Consequences: International Differences in Work-Related Values*, Beverly Hills, CA, Sage.

Hofstede, G. (1991) *Culture and Organizations: Software of the Mind*, New York, McGraw-Hill.

Hopkins, D. (1987) *Improving the Quality of Schooling*, Lewes, Falmer Press.

Hopkins, D. (1994a) 'School Improvement in an ERA of change', in Ribbins, P. and Burridge, E. (eds.) *Improving Education: Promoting Quality in Schools*, London, Cassell.

Hopkins, D. (1994b) 'Yellow brick road', *Managing Schools Today*, March, pp. 14–17.

Hopkins, D. (1996a) 'Unravelling the complexities of school improvement: an overview of the "Improving the Quality of Education for All" (IQEA) Project', paper prepared for the American Educational Research Association Annual Meeting, April.

Hopkins, D. (1996b) 'Towards a theory for school improvement', in Gray, J., Reynolds, D., Fitz-Gibbon, C. and Jesson, D. (eds.) *Merging Traditions: The Future of School Effectiveness and School Improvement*, London, Cassell.

House, E. (1981) 'Three perspectives on innovation', in Lehming, R. and Kane, M. (eds.) *Improving Schools: Using What We Know*, Beveley Hills, CA, Sage.

Hoyle, E. (1981) 'The process of management', in *E323 Management and the School*, Milton Keynes, Open University Press.

Huberman, M. (1990) 'Linkage between researchers and practitioners: a qualitative study', *American Educational Research Journal*, Vol. 27, no. 2, pp. 363–91.

Hughes, M. (1984) 'Educational administration; pure or applied', *Studies in Educational Administration*, Vol. 35, no. 1, pp. 1–10.

Hughes, M. (1985) 'Theory and practice in educational management', in Hughes, M., Ribbins, P. and Thomas, H. (eds.) *Managing Education: The System and the Institution*, London, Holt, Rinehart & Winston.

Hughes, M. (1989) 'Leadership in professionally staffed organisations', in Glatter, R., Preedy, M., Riches, C. and Masterton, M. (eds.) *Understanding School Management*, Milton Keynes, Open University Press.

Hughes, M. and Bush, T. (1991) 'Theory and research as catalysts for change', in Walker, W., Farquhar, R. and Hughes, M. (eds) *Advancing Education: School Leadership in Action*, London, Falmer Press.

Hutchinson, B. (1993) 'The effective reflective school: visions and pipe-dreams in development planning', *Educational Management and Administration*, Vol. 21, no.1., pp. 4–18.

Jayne, E. (1998) 'Effective school development planning', in Middlewood, D. and Lumby, J. (eds.) *Strategic Management in Schools and Colleges*, London, Paul Chapman Publishing.

Jennings, Z. (1994) 'Innovations in Caribbean school systems: why some have become institutionalised and others have not', *Curriculum Studies*, Vol. 2, no. 3. pp. 309–31.

Jirasinghe, D. and Lyons, G. (1996), *The Competent Head: A Job Analysis of Heads' Tasks and Personality Factors*, London, Falmer Press.

Joyce, B. (1991) 'The doors to school improvement' *Educational Leadership*, May, pp. 59–62.

Juran, J. (1989) *Juran on Leadership for Quality*, New York, Free Press.

Lee, J.C.-K. and Walker, A. (1997) 'Managing curriculum programmes and process: towards a whole-school approach', *Curriculum*, Vol. 18, no. 2, pp. 97–105.

Leithwood, K.A. (1992) 'The move toward transformational leadership', *Educational Leadership*, February, pp. 68–72.

Leithwood, K., Tomlinson, D. and Genge, M. (1996) 'Transformational school leadership', in Leithwoood, K. *et al.* (eds.) *International Handbook of Educational Leadership and Administration*, Dordrecht, Kluwer Academic.

Levačić, R. (1995) *Local Management of Schools: Analysis and Practice*, Buckingham, Open University Press.

Levine, D. and Lezotte, L. (1990) *Unusually Effective Schools: A Review and Analysis of Research and Practice*, Madison, WI, National Center for Effective Schools Research and Development.

Lewis, J. (1997) 'From a blank sheet of paper', in Davies, B. and West-Burnham, J. (eds.) *Reengineering and Total Quality in Schools*, London, Pitman Publishing.

Limb, A. (1992) 'Managing colleges into the next century', in Bennett, N., Crawford, M. and Riches, C. (eds.) *Managing Change in Education*, London, Paul Chapman Publishing.

Louis, S.K. and Miles, M.B. (1990) *Improving the Urban High School*, New York, Teachers College Press.

Lumby, J. (1998) 'Strategic planning in further education', in Middlewood, D. and Lumby, J. (eds.) *Strategic Management in Schools and Colleges*, London, Paul Chapman Publishing.

Lumby, J. (1999) 'Strategic planning in further education: the business of values', *Educational Management and Administration*, Vol. 27, no. 1, pp. 71–83.

MacGilchrist, B. and Mortimore, P. (1997) 'The impact of school development plans in primary schools', *School Effectiveness and School Improvement*, Vol. 8, no. 2, pp. 198–218.

Marsh, D. (1992) *Leadership and its Functions in Further and Higher Education*, Mendip Paper MP 035, Bristol, The Staff College.

Marsh, J. (1992) *The Quality Toolkit*, Bedford, IFS.

Middlewood, D. (1998) Strategic management in education: an overview, in Middlewood, D. and Lumby, J. (eds) op. cit.

Middlewood, D. and Lumby, J. (eds.) (1998) *Strategic Management in Schools and Colleges*, London, Paul Chapman Publishing.

Millett, A. (1996) 'A head is more than a manager', *The Times Educational Supplement*, 15 July.

Morgan, G. (1986) *Images of Organization*, Newbury Park, CA, Sage.

Morgan, C., Hall, V. and Mackay, H. (1983) *The Selection of Secondary School Headteachers*, Milton Keynes, Open University Press.

Mortimore, P., Sammons, P., Stoll, L., Lewis, D. and Ecob, R. (1988) *School Matters: The Junior Years*, Wells, Open Books.

Mortimore, P., Sammons, P., Stoll, L., Lewis, D. and Ecob, R. (1986) *The Junior School Project: A Summary of the Main Report*, London, Inner London Education Authority.

Mortimore, P. (1992) 'Issues in school effectiveness' in Reynolds, D. and Cattance, P. (eds.) *School Effectiveness Research, Policy and Practice*, London, Cassell.

Mortimore, P. and Whitty G. (1997) *Can School Improvement Overcome the Effects of Disadvantage?*, London, University of London.

Northfield, J. (1992) 'Leadership to promote quality in learning', in Duignan, P.A. and Macpherson, R.J.S. (eds.) *Educative Leadership: A Practical Theory for New Administrators and Managers*, London, Falmer Press.

Ofsted (1994) 'Framework for the inspection of schools', in *Handbook for the Inspection of Schools*, London, HMSO.

O'Neill, J. (1994) 'Organisational structure and culture', in Bush, T. and West-Burnham, J. (eds.) *The Principles of Educational Management*, Harlow, Longman.

Ozga, J. (ed.) (1993) *Women in Educational Management*, Buckingham, Open University Press.

Reynolds, D. (1982) 'The search for effective schools', *School Organisation*, Vol. 2, no. 3, pp. 215–37.

Reynolds, D. (1992) 'School effectiveness and school improvement: an updated review of the British literature', in Reynolds, D. and Cuttance, P. (eds.) *School Effectiveness: Research, Policy and Practice*, London, Cassell.

Reynolds, D. (1996) 'The problem of the ineffective school: some evidence and some speculations', in Gray, J., Reynolds, D., Fitz-Gibbon, C. and Jesson, D. (eds.) *Merging Traditions: The Future of Research on School Effectiveness and School Improvement*, London, Cassell.

Reynolds, D. and Creemers, B. (1990) 'School effectiveness and school improvement: a mission statement', *School Effectiveness and School Improvement*, Vol. 1, no. 1, pp. 1–3.

Reynolds, D., Hopkins, D. and Stoll, L. (1993) 'Linking school effectiveness knowledge and school improvement practice: towards a synergy', *School Effectiveness and School Improvement*, Vol. 4, no. 1, pp. 37–58.

Reynolds, D., Sammons, P., Stoll, L., Barber, M. and Hillman, J. (1996) 'School effectiveness and school improvement in the United Kingdom', *School Effectiveness and School Improvement*, Vol. 4, no. 2, pp. 133–58.

Riley, K. (1997) 'Quality and equality: competing or complementary objectives?', in Preedy, M., Glatter, R. and Levacic, R. (eds.) *Educational Management: Strategy, Quality and Resources*, Buckingham, Open University Press.

Rozenholtz, S.J. (1989) *Teachers' Workplaces: The Social Organization of Schools*, New York, Longman.

Rutter, M., Maughan, B., Mortimore, P. and Ouston, J. (1979) *Fifteen Thousand Hours – Secondary Schools and their Effects on Children*, London, Open Books.

Sammons, P., Hillman, J. and Mortimore, P. (1995) *Key Characteristics of Effective Schools: A Review of School Effectiveness Research*, London, a report by the Institute of Education for the Office for Standards in Education.

Sammons, P., Thomas, S., Mortimore, P., Owen, C., Pennell, H. and Hillman, J. (1994) *Assessing School Effectiveness: Developing Measures to Put School Performance in Context*, London a report for the Office for Standards in Education, University of London, Institute of Education.

Schein, V.E. (1994) 'Managerial sex typing: a persistent and pervasive barrier to women's opportunities', in Davidson, M.J. and Burke, R.J. (eds.) *Women in Management: Current Research Issues*, London, Paul Chapman Publishing.

Schmuck, P.A. (1986) 'School management and administration: an analysis by gender', in Hoyle, E. and McMahon, A. (eds.) *The Management of Schools: World Yearbook of Education 1986*, London, Kogan Page.

Schmuck, P.A. (1996) 'Women's place in educational administration: past, present and future', in

Leithwood, K. *et al.* (eds.) *International Handbook of Educational Leadership and Administration*, Dordrecht, Kluwer Academic.

Schon, D. A. (1984) 'Leadership as reflection-in-action', in Sergiovanni, T. and Corbally, J. (eds.) *Leadership and Organizational Culture*, Urbana, IL, and Chicago, IL, University of Illinois Press.

Sealy, G. (1992) 'The task of the primary school principal in Barbados', unpublished MEd dissertation, University of Birmingham.

Sergiovanni, T.J. (1984a) 'Leadership as Cultural Expression', in Sergiovanni, T. and Corbally, J. (eds.) *Leadership and Organizational Culture*, Urbana, IL, and Chicago, IL, University of Illinois Press.

Sergiovanni, T.J. (1984b) 'Leadership and excellence in schooling', *Educational Leadership*, February, pp. 4–13.

Sergiovanni, T.J. (1991) *The Principalship: A Reflective Practice Perspective*, Boston, MA, Allyn & Bacon.

Sergiovanni, T.J. (1998) 'Leadership as pedagogy, capital development and school effectiveness', *International Journal of Leadership in Education*, Vol. 1, no. 1, pp. 37–46.

Shakeshaft, C. (1989) *Women in Educational Administration*, Newbury Park, CA, Sage.

Shaw, K.E., Badrik, A.A.M.A. and Hukul, A. (1995) 'Management concerns in the United Arab Emirates state schools', *International Journal of Educational Management*, Vol. 9, no. 4, pp. 8–13.

Simkins, T., Garrett, V., Memon, M. and Ali, R.N. (1998) 'The role perceptions of government and non-government headteachers in Pakistan', *Educational Management and Administration*, Vol. 26, no. 2, pp. 131–45.

Sisum, C. (1997) 'School improvement – translation from theory into practice', in Davies, B. and West-Burnham, J. (eds.) *Reengineering and Total Quality in Schools*, London, Pitman Publishing.

Skelton, M., Reeves, G. and Playfoot, D. (1991) *Development Planning for Primary Schools*, London, Routledge.

Smith, D. and Tomlinson, D. (1989) *The School Effect: A Study of Multi-Racial Comprehensives*, London, Policy Studies Institute.

Smith, R.E. (1996) 'The role of the head of department in "New" British universities', unpublished Ed D thesis, University of Leicester.

Steyn, G.M. and Squelch, J. (1994) 'South African principals' perceptions on restructuring schools: a small-scale evaluation', *School Organisation*, Vol. 14, no. 2, pp. 181–93.

Stoll, L. and Fink, D. (1996) *Changing our Schools: Linking School Effectiveness and School Improvement*, Buckingham, Open University Press.

Stott, K., and Walker, A. (1992) 'The nature and use of mission statements in Singaporean schools', *Educational Management and Administration*, Vol. 20, no. 1, pp. 49–57.

Tannenbaum, R. and Schmidt, W.H. (1973) 'How to choose a leadership pattern', *Harvard Business Review*, May–June, pp. 162–80.

Taylor, A. and Hill, F. (1997) 'Quality management in education', in Harris, A., Bennett, N. and Preedy, M. (eds.) *Organizational Effectiveness and Improvement in Education*, Buckingham, Open University Press.

Teddlie, C. and Stringfield, S. (1993) *Schools Make a Difference: Lessons Learned from a 10 Year Study of School Effects*, New York, Teachers College Press.

Thomas, H. and Martin, J. (1996) *Managing Resources for School Improvement: Creating a Cost-Effective School*, London, Routledge.

Torrington, D. and Weightman, J. (1989) *The Reality of School Management*, Oxford, Blackwell Education.

TTA (1998) *National Standards for Headteachers*, London, Teacher Training Agency.

Van Velzen, W.G., Miles, M.B., Ekholm, N., Hameyer, U. and Robin, D. (eds.) (1985) *Making School Improvement Work*, Leaven, Acco.

Walberg, H. (1991) 'Improving school science in advanced and developing countries', *Review of Educational Research*, Vol. 61, no. 1, pp. 25–69.

Walker, A. and Cheng, Y.C. (1996) 'Professional development in Hong Kong primary schools: beliefs, practices and change', *Journal of Education for Teaching*, Vol. 22, no. 2, pp. 197–212.

Wallace, M. (1989) 'Towards a collegiate approach to curriculum management in primary and middle schools', in Preedy, M. (ed.) *Approaches to Curriculum Management*, Milton Keynes, Open University Press.

Wallace, M. (1991) 'Flexible planning: a key to the management of multiple innovations', *Educational*

Management and Administration, Vol. 19, no. 3, pp. 180–92.

Wallace, M. and Hall, V. (1994) *Inside the SMT*, London, Paul Chapman Publishing.

Weindling, D. (1997) 'Strategic planning in schools: some practical techniques', in Preedy, M., Glatter, R. and Levacic, R. (eds.) *Educational Management: Strategy, Quality, and Resources*, Buckingham, Open University Press.

West-Burnham, J. (1992) *Managing Quality in Schools*, Harlow, Longman.

West-Burnham, J. (1994a) 'Inspection, evaluation and quality assurance', in Bush, T. and West-Burnham, J. (eds.) *The Principles of Educational Management*, Harlow, Longman.

West-Burnham, J. (1994b) 'Strategy, policy and planning', in Bush, T. and West-Burnham, J. (eds.) *The Principles of Educational Management, Harlow*, Longman.

West-Burnham, J. (1994c) 'Management in educational organizations', in Bush, T. and West-Burnham, J. (eds.) *The Principles of Educational Management*, Harlow, Longman.

West-Burnham, J. (1995) *Total Quality Management in Education*, Leicester, University of Leicester, EMDU.

West-Burnham, J. (1997) 'Leadership for learning – reengineering "mind sets"', *School Leadership and Management*, Vol. 17, no. 2, pp. 231–44.

West-Burnham, J., Bush, T., O'Neill, J. and Glover, D. (1995) *Leadership and Strategic Management*, London, Pitman Publishing.

Wong, E.K.P., Sharpe, F. and McCormick, J. (1998), 'Factors affecting the perceived effectiveness of planning in Hong Kong self-managing schools', *Educational Management and Administration*, Vol. 26, no. 1. pp. 67–81.

Yair, G. (1997) 'When classrooms matter: implications of between-classroom variability for educational policy in Israel', *Assessment in Education*, Vol. 4, no. 2, pp. 225–48.

Author Index

Subject Index